Enchantment of the World

THAILAND

By Sylvia McNair

Consultant for Thailand: Herbert P. Phillips, Ph.D., Professor of Anthropology, University of California, Berkeley, California

Consultant for Reading: Robert L. Hillerich, Ph.D., Bowling Green State University, Bowling Green, Ohio

CHILDRENS PRESS ®

CHICAGO

A flower vendor at the floating market

Library of Congress Cataloging-in-Publication Data

McNair, Sylvia.
  Thailand.

  (Enchantment of the world)
  Includes index.
  Summary: Explores the geography, history, arts,
religion, and everyday life of Thailand.
  1. Thailand—Juvenile literature. [1. Thailand]
I. Title. II. Series.
DS563.5.M36 1987   959.3   86-29933
ISBN 0-516-02792-1

Childrens Press, Chicago
Copyright ©1987 by Regensteiner Publishing Enterprises, Inc.
All rights reserved. Published simultaneously in Canada.
Printed in the United States of America.
1 2 3 4 5 6 7 8 9 10 R 96 95 94 93 92 91 90 89 88 87

Picture Acknowledgments
© **Cameramann International, Ltd.**—8 (right), 10 (left), 15,
23 (right), 30 (right), 33 (top left), 38, 58, 63, 73 (bottom
right), 74, 84, 86, 88 (left), 90 (right), 97, 104 (bottom
right), 107 (left), 108
© **Joan Dunlop**—12, 18, 20 (left), 23 (left), 33 (bottom), 40,
57 (right), 71 (left), 90 (left), 94 (right), 107 (right)

EKM Nepenthe: © **Kurt Thorson**—29 (right), 54, 78
(right), 88 (right)
© **Chandler Forman**—5, 95, 102
Gartman Agency: © **Christy Volpe**—32 (bottom)
Historical Pictures Service—44, 45, 47, 48, 49, 50, 51
Image Finders: © **Alice Osinski**—43
Nawrocki Stock Photo: © **D. K. Hulcher**—8 (left), 30 (left),
66, 69, 71 (right), 92; © **D. J. Variakojis**—57 (left), 100;
© **Ulrike Welsch**—20 (right), 53 (2 photos), 87
Odyssey Productions: © **Robert Frerck**—26 (bottom), 33
(top right), 113
Chip & Rosa Maria Peterson: © **Don & Meg Arnosti**—4,
17 (left), 25, 28, 60, 77, 93 (left), 98, 104 (left)
Photo Source International—Cover, 83
Photri—22, 29 (left), 85 (2 photos)
H. Armstrong Roberts: 78 (left), 93 (right);
© **Camerique**—26 (top); © **A. Hubrich**—36; © **Koene**—11
Roloc Color Slides—61, 76, 103
Root Resources: © **Vic Banks/SITES**—10 (right), 59
(2 photos), 68 (right), 94 (left); © **Byron Crader**—96 (left);
© **Kenneth W. Fink**—9; © **Irene Hubbell**—6; © **Jane H.
Kriete**—101; © **Mike Mitrakul**—79; © **Ruth Welty**—68 (left)
© **Bob and Ira Spring**—35, 104 (top right)
Tom Stack and Associates: © **Mickey Gibson**—17 (right),
19, 75, 96 (right); © **Robert McKenzie**—80
Third Coast: © **Jim Kissinger**—110, © **T. Lemke**—73
(top left and right, bottom left)
Wide World Photos—21, 32 (top), 52, 64, 109
Len Meents: Maps on pages 18, 21, 22, 25
Courtesy Flag Research Center, Winchester, MA 01890:
Flag on back cover
Cover: Wat Phra Keo, Bangkok

Young novices at the Temple of the Emerald Buddha in Bangkok

TABLE OF CONTENTS

Chapter 1
LAND OF THE FREE

There was once a wise king who lived in a far-off land where the sun shone brightly over a fertile land. Rains nourished rich fields of grain, the branches of trees were heavy with a hundred kinds of fruit, and the rivers teemed with fish. The king was kind, the land was bountiful, and the people were free and happy.

So goes a thirteenth-century description of the reign of Ramkhamhaeng, the wise and powerful ruler of Sukhothai. Sukhothai was the name of the first independent Thai kingdom, and it means "Dawn of Happiness." Though Thailand has had a rocky history since the days of Sukhothai, this spirit of happiness pervades the Thais' traditional view of their realm.

Colors are brilliant everywhere in Thailand. Flowers bloom in endless array. People wear clothing decorated with intricate embroidery or made of shiny silks woven in stripes of gold, shocking pink, and electric blue. Temples and shrines and palaces glitter in the hot sun.

This is the same country that was called Siam for many years. The present name in the Thai language is *Muang Thai*. The word *thai* means "free." Thus Thailand means, literally, "Land of the Free."

Opposite page: The Grand Palace, Bangkok

Left: An elephant takes the bus lane on a Bangkok thoroughfare.
Right: A water buffalo cart near a village on the Mekong River

CITY AND COUNTRY

In most countries of the world, stark contrasts exist between big-city life and village life. This is also true in Thailand. Here, however, there is only one really large city: Bangkok. Thailand's capital, as well as its major economic and cultural center, Bangkok has a population of almost six million people.

Bangkok is huge, crowded, noisy, and modern. Its residents live in a world of international corporations, towering air-conditioned hotels, theaters, museums, nightclubs, designer shops, pizza parlors, and hamburger joints. The city teems with open-air markets and Buddhist temples, and during rush hour the traffic comes to a virtual gridlock.

Village life, on the other hand, goes on at a fairly slow, relaxed pace. Traditions are strong, old customs still survive. But Thailand is a small country, and the city influence is felt more and more everywhere. Many young people come to Bangkok for higher education or to find jobs—if not permanently, at least for a few months when they are not needed on the farm.

The clouded leopard inhabits the forests of Southeast Asia. Its numbers are declining now due to hunting and the clearing of forests.

FAUNA AND FLORA

Two animals have traditionally been very important as working beasts in Thailand: the elephant and the water buffalo. There are millions of water buffaloes and oxen in the country; elephants number only in the thousands. The water buffalo population is decreasing rapidly, however, as they are slaughtered for meat or replaced by the "iron buffalo," or tractor. The number of wild elephants has decreased seriously in recent years, too.

A few tigers, leopards, and big Himalayan bears are seen in the forested mountains of northern Thailand. Monkeys cavort among the trees and swim in streams in several regions.

Flying squirrels and flying lizards share the rain forests of peninsular Thailand with panthers, deer, and gibbons. Crocodiles prowl the waterways. There are more than fifty species of snakes in this hot and humid jungle, and more than a dozen of them are poisonous. Less frightening creatures are the five hundred kinds of butterflies and dozens of gorgeous tropical birds.

9

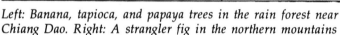

Left: Banana, tapioca, and papaya trees in the rain forest near Chiang Dao. Right: A strangler fig in the northern mountains

The virgin rain forests of south Thailand are so fertile that as many as a hundred different kinds of trees can exist on a single acre. Among them are rubber trees, bamboo, screw pines, and others ranging in height from dwarf-size to giant. Vines and plants climb the trunks; mosses, fungi, and hundreds of varieties of orchids take root on logs.

Of course, life is not perfect for everyone in Thailand. There are many very poor people, just as there are in every country. The great majority of the people are farmers, and not all of the land is fertile. In some regions it is very hard to make a living from the land, and people must turn to other occupations.

Unstable political conditions and military conflicts in some of Thailand's neighboring countries cause problems, particularly when large numbers of refugees spill across the borders.

Kampuchean refugees waiting for rice in a refugee camp near the Thailand-Kampuchea border

But several factors have contributed to a greater degree of unity and stability in Thailand than in certain other Asian nations.

Thai culture is solidly rooted in a strong sense of family. In the villages, a family is a large unit, consisting not just of parents and children, but often including grandparents and other relatives, all living together in a single house or cluster of houses.

Another important influence is religion. Ninety-five percent of Thai citizens are Buddhists, and this is a religion that teaches tolerance, generosity, and serenity.

So the Thai people do have much to smile about. A land and climate that are generally kind, a way of life that emphasizes personal freedom, a tradition of family security and love, and a benign religion—all these influences have shaped the character of the people.

Chapter 2

THE LAND AND
THE PEOPLE

People have lived in Southeast Asia for thousands of years. Archaeologists have found evidence that a rather highly developed Bronze Age culture existed here as early as four thousand years ago. Some experts think it may be the world's oldest bronze culture civilization.

We do not know who the first people to live in this corner of Southeast Asia were, but we do know that many different groups came here over the centuries. Some of the earliest ones were the Mons and the Khmers.

More than four out of every five people who live in Thailand today belong to the ethnic group called Thais. They are descendants of people who started migrating south from China some thirteen hundred years ago, probably from China's Szechwan province. There are large pockets of Thais still living in villages of southern China. It is believed that the migration of Thais from China increased rapidly when Kublai Khan, a strong military leader from Mongolia, conquered China in A.D. 1264.

About 10 percent of the citizens of Thailand are of Chinese descent, 4 percent Malaysian. Most of the rest are tribal people who have lived in Thailand for hundreds of years or are people who have come to Thailand from the neighboring countries of Laos, Cambodia (Kampuchea), Burma, Vietnam, and India.

Most Thais—about 80 percent of them—are farmers who live in small villages. The people of some of these villages have very little to do with the outside world. They help each other in their farm work, help support their local Buddhist temple and its group of monks, and often organize temple fairs.

The elected head of a village is called a *phujajbaan*. His duties and responsibilities go beyond governing. He also organizes activities that involve the whole community and acts as an informal judge in settling disputes between people.

People of Chinese descent, the second largest group in Thailand, are primarily engaged in merchant trades. Most of them live in Bangkok and other large towns. At the time the Chinese were coming into the area, the Thais had control of farmland and of government administration, so the only way for the newcomers to make a living was in trade.

Many Chinese have integrated into Thai culture. Most have adopted Thai names, and over the years there has been a great deal of intermarriage. As a result many people who consider themselves to be Thai have at least one Chinese ancestor.

A BOUNTIFUL LAND

The climate and the fertile land of Thailand have made life much easier for its people than for those who live in many other parts of the world.

A farmer's home and a field of rice seedlings

Among the blessings are plenty of sunshine, abundant rainfall, rich soil, year-round pleasant temperatures, and many rivers and streams filled with fish. Getting enough to eat has never been difficult in most parts of the country.

Except for floods in certain areas, natural disasters are almost nonexistent here. Unlike many other less fortunate areas, Thailand does not have to worry about earthquakes, typhoons, and volcanic eruptions. Houses can be fairly simple and inexpensive, as they don't have to withstand severe weather.

Because Thais have not had to struggle as hard as some other people, they have developed a relaxed and peaceful outlook on life. Trade with other countries started early here, for two reasons: it was easy to produce surplus stores of food, and the country was located at a crossroads between the Chinese and Indian empires, with easy access by boat along the waterways.

Some Thais say that the odd shape of their country resembles the head of an elephant. Perhaps this notion came about because elephants have been the most important animal in Thailand's history. Warriors rode elephants into battle in medieval times, and they have been trained as work animals to perform many tasks, such as helping to harvest timber.

To others, the map of Thailand looks more like a flower, with an irregularly-shaped blossom making up the main portion and a long, narrow stem stretching south.

The whole country is about the size of France. About fifty-six million people live here. One out of every ten are in the huge capital city of Bangkok. There are a few other smaller cities, but most Thais live in small villages. Thailand's neighbors are Laos to the north and northeast, Kampuchea (Cambodia) to the east, Malaysia to the south, and Burma to the west. The climate north of the Gulf of Thailand is that of a tropical savanna; the area south of the gulf has a tropical monsoon climate.

There are four main regions of Thailand outside the city of Bangkok and its immediate surroundings: the mountains of the far north, the dry plateau of the northeast, the central plains, and the south. They are quite different from each other, but national pride unites the people of all the regions.

THE MOUNTAINOUS NORTH

Waterfalls tumbling over rocky hills, misty green mountains, secluded valleys, jungles teeming with rare wildlife—this is the exotic and remote northern region of Thailand. The north is probably the most picturesque part of the country, both for its terrain and for its people and their life-styles.

Left: A waterfall in Doi Inthanon National Park near Chiang Mai. Above: A child of the Hmong tribe along an isolated village road in the north

There are some tiny, isolated villages in the north where modern advantages such as schools and clinics are only beginning to exist. Some of the hill people here have never been any farther from their homes than they are able to walk. The only contact some villages have with the outside world is an occasional visit by helicopter from the government's border patrol.

These mountains, many of them more than a mile (1.6 kilometers) high, are southern foothills of the great Himalayan Range, which separates north and central Asia from the warm, moist southeast.

A wildlife sanctuary in this area has been called by a committee of the United Nations "one of the wildlife treasure chests of the world." Several species of monkeys, a herd of wild buffalo, tigers, leopards, many kinds of deer, and a host of rarer and lesser-known animals graze on the open grasslands, roam through groves of bamboo, and climb the forested slopes.

A Hmong villager's home in the northern mountains

There are more than a hundred distinct tribes of seminomadic people who live in the mountains along the borders of Laos and Burma. Some have been so isolated from the rest of the country that their traditions and customs have not changed in hundreds of years. Certain of these traditions present a problem for the government. For example, their method of growing some crops has depleted the soil to a dangerous extent.

A more serious problem is that one of the most lucrative crops grown in this part of Thailand is poppies—the poppies from which the dangerous drug opium is derived. The government declared the growing of this crop illegal some decades ago, but it is very difficult to police the isolated poppy fields.

King Bhumibol has taken a personal interest in the northern region and has put a great deal of effort into teaching the hill

18

Lush orchids adorn shrines and spirit houses throughout Thailand.

tribes both crop rotation and the substitution of other money-making crops for poppies. These efforts may in time put a stop to Thailand's illegal drug traffic.

The north is the coolest part of Thailand. Temperatures can dip down almost to the freezing point. Parts of the region are still rich in timber; this is where trained elephants drag huge logs down the steep slopes to the riverbanks. From here the lumber is floated downriver to mills for processing.

Several kinds of minerals are found in the mountain area, including some of the world's finest sapphires. Farm crops grow in the high fields; cattle graze in broad valleys; orchids grow wild in the hills; lush orchards produce fruit for sale in the cities.

A huge dam in the region generates enough electric power to serve nearly half the nation.

Chiang Mai: An overview of the city (left) and the Phu Ping Palace (right), the summer home of the royal family

Chiang Mai is the major metropolis of the north. It is the largest city in Thailand outside of Bangkok, but its population numbers only around two hundred thousand. There are hundreds of beautiful temples in Chiang Mai; people come from long distances to admire them. Much of the city is still relatively unspoiled and relaxed, although developments to attract tourists threaten the city's traditional beauty. Noisy motorcycles and other small vehicles, along streets that are lined with countless souvenir shops, are evidence that Chiang Mai is no longer isolated from the rest of the world.

THE ARID NORTHEAST

Thailand's northeastern region is, for the most part, a dry and dusty high plateau, separated from the country of Laos by the Mekong River. Nature has been less generous to this part of the

Bangkok

Farmers threshing rice in Surin province in the northeast

country, which the Thais call Issan, than to other areas. The soil is hard to work and not very productive; most of the year brings either too little rain or flood-causing torrents. This is the poorest region of Thailand.

Transportation into the northeast was difficult until quite recently, so not many industries have located there. In the 1950s, a modern road called the Friendship Highway was built with the assistance of the United States. This made it possible for the farmers and small manufacturers of the northeast to get their goods to the markets of Bangkok. Air and rail service is now available to the major towns, also.

Progress is being made in bringing needed facilities to remote villages: roads, electric lines, medical facilities, and agricultural experiment stations. Dams have been built to control floods and provide irrigation for agriculture, and a university has been established.

Bangkok

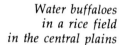

*Water buffaloes
in a rice field
in the central plains*

THE CENTRAL PLAINS

Thailand's heartland is its central plains, where an almost endless sea of rice fields stretches forth as far as one can see.

At the end of the dry season, in late May, farmers come out with their water buffaloes (or, in many places, "iron buffaloes") to plow the hard, cracked earth. Then the fields are flooded and the young rice plants are set out by hand. In June the rains come down and the plants shoot up, nourished by the rich sediment washed down from the northern mountains. Streams and canals stretching out from the major rivers carry water to the rice paddies. In November the rains end abruptly and harvest time approaches.

This is the fertile Chao Phraya basin, where the cycle of rice-growing has repeated itself each year for centuries. The Chao Phraya and its tributaries are to Thailand what the Nile River is to Egypt and the Mississippi to the central United States.

Houses on stilts provide shelter for farm animals.

Historically, it was the main transportation artery from north to south, as well as the source of fertile soil for agriculture.

Farmers in this region are relatively well off. Both crops and the market for rice are quite dependable, and the farmlands are usually handed down in the same family, generation after generation.

While this part of the kingdom has seen more changes, more "modernization," than most of the other regions, people here still live in traditional wooden Thai-style houses. These are built up on stilts to provide living quarters for the farm animals—pigs, chickens, and water buffalo—underneath. The people's villages here are small, and their way of life is much the same as that of their ancestors.

The central plains were the location of Thailand's two ancient capitals, Sukhothai in the north and Ayutthaya in the south. The ruins of these ancient cities tell the story of a powerful, artistically talented, and highly religious people who lived here long ago.

South of Bangkok along the Gulf of Thailand are two regions that have rapidly become popular resort areas. White sand beaches front on sparkling blue waters; coconut palm trees sway with the soft breezes; a lovely coral reef beckons to scuba divers to study the sea life beneath the surface. Small tropical islands lie offshore; inland are waterfalls cascading into clean, cool pools.

Until a few years ago this area was relatively undiscovered; there were only a few tiny fishing villages with small clusters of modest vacation cottages for rent.

Since the 1960s big changes have occurred. Huge luxury hotels with fine restaurants and elaborate sports facilities have been built. One center of this activity is the resort city of Pattaya, on the eastern side of the Gulf of Thailand. The other is Hua Hin, on the western side of the gulf, where the royal family maintains a summer palace.

Along with the sun and sand that draw vacationers are other valuable natural resources; sapphire and ruby mines, an abundance of fine seafood in the gulf, and ideal conditions for the commercial raising of orchids.

THE SOUTH

More sandy beaches are found in the far south of Thailand, where the country forms a narrow isthmus leading to Malaysia. For a part of the way the isthmus is shared with Burma, then it becomes all Thailand territory stretching south to the border of Malaysia. The isthmus lies between the Gulf of Thailand on the east and the Indian Ocean on the west.

This is a region of superb natural beauty, with wild jungles, rocky mountains, powdery white sand, and clear salt water. In

Bangkok

The white beaches, palms, and limestone mountains of one of the many islands off southern Thailand

some spots steep cliffs rise sharply from the waters. During low tides some of the beaches are completely covered with shells.

Despite its obvious attractions, this part of Thailand has not yet been completely taken over by vacation resorts. It seems inevitable that it will be, someday.

There are two rainy seasons in the south, and more rain falls here than in the rest of the country. December and January are the wettest months. The humid climate is perfect for growing rubber and coconut trees, as well as tropical fruits.

At the far southern end of the isthmus, the influence of neighboring Malaysia is obvious. Many people speak Malay as well as Thai, the food is much like that of Malaysia, and many of the residents are Muslim rather than Buddhist.

Above: High-rise buildings give the ancient city of Bangkok a modern skyline.
Below: The Chao Phraya River, Bangkok's major shipping route, flows past homes, temples, and shrines.

Chapter 3
CITY OF THE ANGELS

In the Thai language it is called *Krungthep*, which means "City of the Angels." To the rest of the world, it is known as Bangkok. Capital, financial and cultural center, and the only huge city in Thailand, Bangkok is among the top twenty cities in the world in population. With almost six million people in its metropolitan area, it is about the same size as the entire colony of Hong Kong.

It is also one of the world's noisiest cities; automobiles, trucks, and motorcycles crowd the streets, horns blaring. Most of the vehicles seem to be missing their mufflers. Unique three-wheeled vehicles called "tuk-tuks" race around town carrying passengers—and adding to the din.

Yet just around the corner from a broad avenue filled with a sea of congested motor traffic, a person can stumble onto a calm, tree-shaded tropical garden or a quiet, narrow *klong* (canal).

At one time canals crisscrossed the entire city; they were the city's streets, carrying virtually all the traffic. In recent years many of the old klongs have been paved over, but some are still open. Houses built on stilts line the banks; on the porches a profusion of orchid plants may hang side by side with the family laundry.

Residents along Thailand's canals do their daily shopping at the floating markets.

THE MARKETS

Bangkok has been called the Venice of the East. Despite the decline in the number of klongs, water traffic is still nearly as heavy as street traffic. Activity on the river begins early in the morning, when barges arrive from upriver carrying rice for the mills. Other barges head inland with goods to sell in the villages. Small sampans (long, narrow, canoe-shaped wooden boats) — some propelled by outboard motors, others by oars or poles — maneuver in and out among the larger craft. Men and women from the farms, wearing broad-brimmed straw hats to shade their eyes, steer the sampans. They are bringing fruits, vegetables, and flowers to sell at the famous Floating Market at Thonburi.

Thonburi is part of the capital city's metropolitan area. Actually, it was the capital of the country for fifteen years before King Rama I moved across the river to Bangkok.

Along the route people are getting up to start their day. Adults are standing waist-deep in the klongs, brushing their teeth and taking their morning baths. Little boys interrupt their bathing to

Typical street scenes in Bangkok: A lush produce market (left)
and a row of shoppers' motorcycles (right)

swim up to excursion boats and hitch a ride, clowning around and flashing bright grins at the passengers. Old women with fishing lines watch the morning water parade as they try to catch their breakfast.

Dozens of shops and open-air stalls are crowded together at the riverside market. Vendors in the sampans paddle up to other boat passengers and to the houses along the waterfront, offering an amazing variety of goods for sale. Each house has a landing platform, so deliveries are easily made.

On Saturdays a huge weekend market is set up under canvas awnings on the outskirts of the city. Items for sale range from plants and foods to secondhand books, antiques, caged birds, clothing, handicrafts, and semiprecious stones.

Traditional native markets are only a small part of the commerce carried on in Bangkok. Much more common are modern shopping malls, large department stores, and small, exclusive shops. International shoppers love this city; many locally made items carry very reasonable price tags.

*Above: A girl in Bangkok takes in laundry after
drenching rains have flooded the streets.
Right: A typical Thai movie poster—larger than life*

THE FACE OF BANGKOK

During a heavy rainstorm the water pours down so hard and
fast that pedestrians find themselves wading ankle-deep in
rushing streams that cover the sidewalks—as if the klongs were
trying to recover their territory from the streets. The air is so
warm that residents and tourists alike are able to keep sloshing
along without too much discomfort. However, in certain years,
flooding has risen to waist level for several weeks at a time, and
ordinary activities have simply ceased.

Movie theaters in Bangkok offer shows from all over the world.
Billboard-sized pictures of popular stars advertise current
programs. Movies are a popular form of entertainment, although
home viewing of movies on videocassettes threatens the movie
theater business. Foreign-language films are presented with Thai
subtitles or translations. There is censorship; some movies,
especially the X-rated type, are banned.

Bangkok is a major crossroads of Southeast Asia. East and West meet here. This is particularly evident in the contrasts in architecture. Western-style glass-and-steel skyscrapers, huge international hotels, and modern shopping centers crowd close to Buddhist temples and ornate palaces.

Many residents of Bangkok live in what are called "shop houses." The ground floor houses a store, small factory, or other business, while the upper floors are living quarters for the business owner's family. But the more picturesque old-style Thai home survives in many neighborhoods—especially along the waterways.

Thai homes come in many sizes and shapes and are built of different kinds of materials. One type found in Bangkok is made of wood, usually unpainted, and built on stilts to keep the family dry during the rainy season. Some of the rooms are quite small, but they seem more spacious because they are not crowded with furniture. Roofs are steep, and pointed decorations rise atop the gables. There is usually a large veranda; porches and walkways of varying width may occur at more than one level. Often more than one structure is included in a group of dwellings; the additional ones are used by servants or relatives of the owner.

OLD BANGKOK

The oldest part of Bangkok is within an arch of the Chao Phraya River. Here is where the present dynasty's first king, Rama I, built his Grand Palace. The king who rules today lives in a more modern palace in another part of the city, and the Grand Palace is used only for royal ceremonies. Some of the reception rooms are open to the public.

Above: Bangkok's Grand Palace is a walled complex of numerous ornate structures. One of them
is the king's residence (below), where Thailand's king performs many of his official duties.

Above: Democracy Monument, on Bangkok's Rajdamnoen Avenue (left); typical stilt houses along a klong (canal) in Bangkok (right). Below: Lower-income dwellings in Bangkok huddle beneath a backdrop of modern buildings.

The palace compound has been changed and expanded many times since Rama I's days. Today it is a wonderland of spires, rooftops with corners that sweep upward in graceful points, elegant gates, tiny shrines, and temples. The architecture of the various structures is a mixture—some are uniquely Thai, some are similar to Victorian-era buildings of the Western world.

One small shrine contains a stone pillar. King Rama I placed it there as a symbolic cornerstone of his reign, and all distances in Bangkok are measured from this stone. He also constructed the most precious of all Thai shrines, the Royal Chapel of the Emerald Buddha.

The origin of the Emerald Buddha is unknown, but it was found in Chiang Mai in the fifteenth century. When found, it was covered with stucco and gold leaf. Later the stucco flaked off, and the beautiful green stone of the original statue was revealed.

The Buddha is actually made of jasper, not emerald, but the statue is very valuable and special to the Thai people. It is looked upon as the national *palladium*, a word that means champion or protector. Thai people swear oaths on the Emerald Buddha as Christians do on the Bible, and no one would dare go back on such an oath.

Murals within the small but magnificent chapel depict scenes from Buddha's life. Some of the panels of the doors are inlaid with mother-of-pearl.

The Chapel of the Emerald Buddha is within the Wat Phra Keo, adjacent to the palace. The word *wat* means monastery, but Buddhist monasteries in Thailand are much more than homes for monks. They are community centers for all kinds of activities; they are museums, libraries, learning centers, and in many places homes for the aged and the orphaned.

The magnificent Reclining Buddha in the Wat Po Temple is 160 feet (48.8 meters) long.

Wat Phra Keo is the royal temple, where the king performs his religious duties. Within its compound are many shrines, pavilions, and other structures, whose walls sparkle with paint, brightly colored tiles, and precious stones. Elegant gates, imposing statues, murals, and gilded spires create a scene that dazzles the eyes.

The largest temple complex within the Grand Palace area is the Wat Po, containing a reclining Buddha 160 feet (49 meters) long.

Three other wats in Bangkok are worth mentioning. Wat Trimit houses a 10-foot (3-meter) statue of Buddha cast of 5.5 tons (4,990 kilograms) of solid gold. Wat Benchambopit, the Marble Temple, is a more modern and very beautiful structure. In its courtyard are more than fifty statues of Buddha. Wat Saket, containing one of the largest bronze Buddhas in Thailand, is at the base of the Golden Mount, a graceful spire that can be seen from almost anywhere in the city.

The ruins of the ancient city of Sukhothai

Chapter 4
THREE DYNASTIES

The history of Thailand has been characterized as a chronicle of its kings. Fortunately, many of Thailand's kings have been progressive, farsighted, well educated, and compassionate. Even today, when the present ruler, King Bhumibol, has far less power than the absolute and divine right accorded to his predecessors, the monarchy provides a great deal of thoughtful leadership to the nation.

Thailand is the only nation in Southeast Asia that has never been a colony of any European power. That is why the nation that was known to the rest of the world for many centuries as Siam now calls itself Thailand, Land of the Free.

SUKHOTHAI—"DAWN OF HAPPINESS"

The documented history of Thailand begins when the independent kingdom was founded in 1238. The capital of this kingdom was Sukhothai, a city in the north central part of the country. The first king was named Sri Indradit.

King Ramkhamhaeng developed the elegant Thai alphabet and writing system.

The Sukhothai period lasted only about two hundred years, but it was a most important time in history. Eight kings ruled during this period. The most famous of these was King Ramkhamhaeng, son of the first ruler. He was head of state from 1275 to 1317, and he achieved many long-lasting benefits for his country.

In those days a leader had to be strong and successful in battle in order to hold the respect of his people, as many groups throughout the area frequently waged war on each other. Elephants were used in battle, and King Ramkhamhaeng was especially skillful in the use of war elephants.

In Thailand the history of King Ramkhamhaeng's reign in Sukhothai has an idealized quality much like that described in the legends of King Arthur at Camelot. However, unlike Camelot, there actually was a Sukhothai.

Ramkhamhaeng's most lasting and important achievement was the development of the Thai alphabet and writing system. He borrowed from the script of the Khmer people to create his graceful Thai letters.

The arts were encouraged during this period, too. The king brought Chinese artisans into the kingdom to teach his subjects how to make fine porcelain. He invited Buddhist monks from Ceylon to visit and to preach, and he made Hinayana Buddhism the dominant practice of his country. A new type of architecture was created, characterized by many levels of roofs tapering upward toward the sky. The king supported the building of beautiful temples. Statues of Buddha from this period are elegant, with a long body and smiling face.

King Ramkhamhaeng had a strong feeling of responsibility for his subjects. Common people were encouraged to bring their grievances directly to him. A bell was hung by the palace gate, to be rung by citizens who wanted to speak with their ruler.

A stone pillar erected in the year 1292 in Sukhothai is still there among the ruins of the ancient city, and the Thai people like to quote the words engraved on it. They describe the reign of King Ramkhamhaeng the Great as it is remembered in Thai history:

> This Sukhothai is good. In the water there are fish. In the fields there is rice. The king does not levy a rate [tax] on his people. . . . Who wants to trade in elephants, trades. Who wants to trade in horses, trades. Who wants to trade in gold and silver, trades. . . ."

AYUTTHAYA

Later kings of Sukhothai were not as powerful and did not accomplish as much as Ramkhamhaeng the Great. Eventually the kingdom was overcome by one of Sukhothai's princes. This prince, later known as King Ramathibodi, founded a new kingdom in 1350. He set up his capital south of Sukhothai and up the Chao Phraya River from where Bangkok is today.

The ruins of Ayutthaya

Ayutthaya, the new capital, was built on an island at the confluence of three rivers. This kingdom was in power for four hundred years.

Ramathibodi was successful in bringing together the people from different parts of Southeast Asia who lived in the Chao Phraya basin. Some Chinese and Indians had come on their own, but there were also Laotian, Malay, Khmer, Burmese, and Vietnamese people who had been captured in battle. Most, however, were Thai. During Ramathibodi's reign, all of these people were absorbed into the Ayutthaya society.

The first king of Ayutthaya organized an efficient government and established a system of laws. The kingdom he founded lasted for 417 years, with a succession of thirty-three kings. It was a period of many battles with neighboring people, during which Ayutthaya grew stronger and stronger. At its peak, it held control over large areas of Southeast Asia, including parts of Burma and the Malay peninsula.

The religion of Ayutthaya, like Sukhothai before, was primarily Buddhist but with some Hindu influences. Kings were believed to have a divine right to rule. When they were crowned, they were given the names of Hindu gods, and in time they were regarded as gods themselves.

As gods, the kings had absolute power. They owned all the land and everything on the land. They could do as they pleased with the taxes levied on their subjects. Royal palaces were lavishly decorated, as they represented the homes of gods.

In 1454 King Trailok introduced some reforms. He gave control of much of the land to important government and military officials. The more important the official was, the more land was awarded to him. While the king still held legal ownership, the officials had the authority to levy taxes on anything produced by people who lived on their land. The official was permitted to keep part of these revenues; the rest he turned over to the royal treasury.

The subjects paid their taxes in cash, food products, or precious metals. A frequent alternative was *corvée* labor, by which unpaid work could be given in place of money or food.

Taxes were used to finance the royal government, to wage war, to pay bureaucrats, and to build public facilities, such as monasteries, roads, and canals.

During long periods of peace, prosperity increased and arts and crafts developed. Skilled artists created chinaware, swords, jewelry, and gold objects. Thai monasteries and temples dating from this period are spectacularly beautiful. Sculptors and painters lavished their attention and genius on these public buildings, which were village centers where all kinds of community events were held.

The Ayutthaya period was one in which the small kingdoms of the Chao Phraya basin were united, and interaction with other Asian countries grew. Diplomats and scholars were exchanged, and trading was carried on in such products as teak, salt, spices, and hides. Relationships with China became especially strong.

Europeans arrived in Ayutthaya in the sixteenth century. The first were the Portuguese, who came in 1512. Four years later they signed a treaty, agreeing to furnish arms to Ayutthaya in return for the freedom to trade, reside, and practice their own religion in Thai territory.

Peaceful times were often interrupted by border wars with Burma. For a short period of time in the late 1500s, Ayutthaya was a subject of Burma.

During this time, a nine-year-old prince of Ayutthaya was captured and taken to Burma as a hostage. The Burmese king took an interest in him and personally taught him the martial arts. He expected that when the prince grew up he could be put on the throne of Ayutthaya as a docile puppet of Burma.

It didn't work out that way. The prince is remembered as King Naresuen the Great, the most important warrior-king in Thai history. He returned to Ayutthaya at the age of sixteen, where he raised an army and fought off invaders from the east, awaiting his chance to become king. In 1584 he declared Thai independence, and six years later he succeeded his father as king. For three years he fought against Burmese invaders. Finally he and the Burmese crown prince faced each other in combat on their war elephants, and King Naresuen killed the prince.

After this, the power of the Burmese grew weaker and weaker, and for the next 160 years they were no longer a threat to Ayutthaya.

This mural and sculpture depict the battle between Ayutthaya's Prince Naresuen and the Burmese crown prince.

Meanwhile, Ayutthaya became more and more an international crossroads, a very cosmopolitan city. Traders from China, Japan, Persia, France, Holland, Spain, England, and Portugal carried on commerce there. Beautiful objects from many countries were imported. The palaces and monasteries were decorated with Persian rugs and lamps and with works of art from China and Japan.

As foreigners were traveling to Ayutthaya, Thai people were discovering the rest of the world at the same time. The first Thai travelers to Europe were members of a delegation sent to The Hague, in Holland, in 1608.

Diplomatic relations were also established with Japan. However, an unfortunate incident in 1632, resulting in the death of some Japanese palace guards, led to a breakdown of Thai-Japanese friendship. Relations were not mended for more than two hundred years.

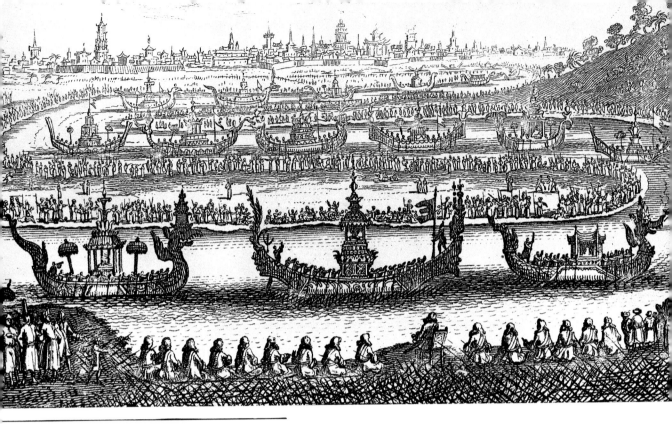

A view of Ayutthaya in the 1700s

In the middle of the seventeenth century, when colonists from Europe were first settling North America, the city of Ayutthaya had a larger population than London, England. It was a walled city, protected by seven fortresses, and sparkling with gilt-trimmed temples dominated by huge golden images of Buddha. Many kinds of boats and ships sailed on the waterways that crisscrossed the metropolis—Chinese junks, Arab dhows, lavishly decorated royal barges, oceangoing sailing ships from Europe, and smaller craft.

King Narai was a ruler who was interested in establishing good relations with France. This was partly because he was wary of the Dutch and wanted an ally in case of problems with them. One of the king's advisers was a Greek adventurer who wanted to convert the king to Christianity. He persuaded Narai to let French missionaries establish a church in Ayutthaya in 1664.

The Thai king receives the ambassador of France's King Louis XIV.

In 1684 the king sent an embassy and some students to France. This was followed by the first French embassy to Ayutthaya, sent by King Louis XIV of France.

Unfortunately, a few years later the Greek adviser led a conspiracy that eventually toppled King Narai. For the next 150 years the Thais were very suspicious of foreigners and tried to keep out Western influence completely.

The kings who followed Narai were weak, and in 1767 the Burmese again invaded Ayutthaya. This time they succeeded in destroying the once-glorious city. Not only were all of the art treasures stolen or damaged beyond repair, but nearly all of the country's historical records were burned as well. Acts of vandalism like this greatly harm our ability to know the past, and the Thai people still bitterly resent this time in their history.

Many of the survivors of the invasion were taken prisoner and carried off to Burma. From a prosperous and important city of more than a million people, as Ayutthaya is reported to have been at its peak, the population was reduced to only about ten thousand people. This means that only one out of every one hundred former residents was left!

Even these few survivors abandoned the ruins eventually, and nature took over, covering most of the remains with vegetation. In recent decades, the government of Thailand has excavated much of the old city and has plans to rebuild many of the ancient temples and palaces.

After the Burmese destroyed Ayutthaya, a Thai general named Phraya Tak founded a new capital city across the river from modern Bangkok. He was crowned as King Taksin, and spent fifteen years reviving a Thai government, driving out the invaders, and unifying the people.

Modern Thai history starts at the end of Taksin's reign, when another general, Chao Phraya Chakri, became the first of a royal dynasty that exists to this day.

BANGKOK AND THE CHAKRI DYNASTY

General Chakri, crowned King Rama I, moved the capital across the Chao Phraya River to Bangkok in 1782. One of his first projects was to build the Grand Palace, a replica of the one in Ayutthaya. He also copied Ayutthaya's island setting by having a canal dug around the city.

Once again, during Rama I's reign, the Burmese invaded Thailand. They were defeated in 1785, and have never again marched against the Thais.

*Mongkut
(Rama IV)*

King Rama II succeeded to the throne in 1809. His fifteen-year reign was a time of peace and prosperity. He was well educated and interested in literature. He encouraged the writing of poetry, and wrote a number of verse-plays himself.

King Rama III (reigned 1824-51) was concerned with the danger of invasion by foreign powers; consequently, he set limits on trade with the West. In contrast, it was during his time that Christian missionaries were once again permitted to come into the country.

King Mongkut (Rama IV, reigned 1851-68) is thought of as the king who brought Thailand into the modern era. Mongkut was very well educated; he had studied Latin, English, mathematics, science, history, and geography. He was forty-eight years old when he became king and had been a Buddhist monk for twenty-six years. During those years he had traveled widely, so he had a very different outlook than had former kings, most of whom had led very secluded lives.

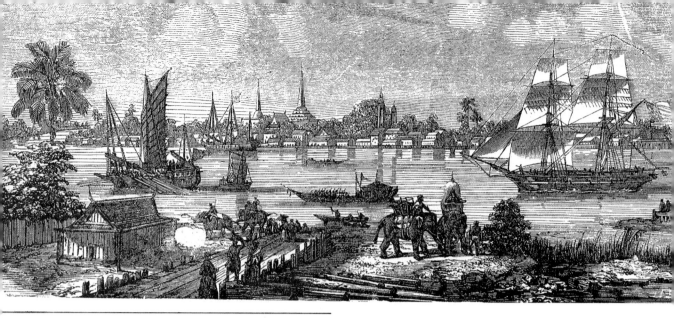

The town and harbor of Bangkok in 1858

Mongkut was intensely interested in Western ideas, and he understood the art of diplomacy. He succeeded in negotiating treaties with many European countries and with the United States. He also established his nation's first mint, modernized the army, and brought in European advisers to reorganize his government administration. Because he recognized the importance of transportation to the economy, he promoted the building of roads and the digging of canals.

Cultural matters were important to Mongkut, too. He encouraged education, especially the study of foreign languages. He was influential in restoring some of the historical records that had been partially destroyed during the destruction of Ayutthaya and in rebuilding deteriorating Buddhist treasures. He corresponded widely, in English, with important people in several foreign countries. During the American Civil War, he even offered President Abraham Lincoln fighting elephants to help in the war.

The book *Anna and the King of Siam* and the musical *The King and I* are patterned on the life of King Mongkut. But these Western fantasies represent totally inaccurate versions of what actually occurred in Thai history.

*Chulalongkorn (Rama V)
in uniform*

Mongkut's son Chulalongkorn, King Rama V, held the throne from 1868 to 1910. He was even more progressive and more interested in learning from the West than his father had been. At the same time, he was determined to resist any foreign domination and to hold onto traditional Thai values.

Chulalongkorn traveled quite a bit in neighboring Asian countries. He made two trips to Europe as well, and sent Thai students to foreign countries to be educated. He followed his father's example by building railroads and establishing postal and telegraph services.

Among the many reforms of Rama V were the total abolition of all forms of slavery and the founding of schools and health centers. Following his father's example, he stayed close to his subjects. He traveled extensively throughout the countryside to observe the living conditions of his subjects firsthand.

Chulalongkorn presents to his subjects the crown prince, Vajiravudh, who will become Rama VI.

Today Chulalongkorn is one of the most highly regarded of all Thai kings, and the anniversary of his death is observed as a national holiday.

King Vajiravudh (Rama VI), Chulalongkorn's son, was educated in England, at Oxford. He, too, was a progressive leader. He expanded educational opportunities and encouraged the participation of Thai people in such international organizations as the Red Cross and the Boy Scouts. He was a writer and a poet.

World War I took place during King Vajiravudh's reign, and he sent a force to Europe to fight on the side of the Allies.

*Prajadhipok
(Rama VII)*

Vajiravudh had no sons, so when he died the throne went to his younger brother, Prajadhipok (Rama VII). Prajadhipok was in power at an unfortunate time, the late 1920s, when his country was suffering from an economic depression. Besides that, he was not as well prepared for his office as his predecessors had been, since he had never expected to become king.

The combination of these unfavorable circumstances led to dissatisfaction among some of the military men and civilians close to the throne, and in 1932 a nonviolent *coup d'état* ended seven hundred years of absolute monarchy in Thailand. Rama VII agreed to a limited monarchy; he served under a constitution until 1935, when he abdicated.

Thai troops at their post during an unsuccessful coup in September 1985

After 1932, power in Thailand was never again exclusively in the hands of the kings. Instead, the royal family serves the country in a ceremonial and advisory capacity, much like England's royalty. The king is the symbol of national unity and of moral authority.

Three major blocks of power emerged: the military, the civilian government officials, and the merchant class.

After the bloodless revolution of 1932, the Thais experimented with various approaches to democracy. Several strong leaders came to the forefront at this time. Political power seesawed back and forth between those with socialist leanings and a more conservative, military-minded group.

During World War II, Japan occupied Thailand and forced its collaboration. Japan declared war against the Allies, but the Thai ambassador to Washington, acting against his government's orders, refused to deliver an official declaration of war. He said it did not represent the will of the majority of the Thais. The United States government believed this to be true. Despite Thailand's declaration of war, the U.S. never considered a real state of war to exist between itself and Thailand.

Left: King Bhumibol (Rama IX)
Above: Queen Sirikit

Thailand's present royal ruler is King Bhumibol, Rama IX, grandson of Rama V. He was born in Boston, Massachusetts, in 1927, while his father was a student at Harvard Medical School. He has been king since 1946, and he and his queen are widely loved and respected.

Democracy as it is known in the West, with changes of administration brought about through peaceful elections, has not yet become the normal way of life in Thailand. Instead, the government has changed hands fairly frequently as a result of coups. Usually, however, these coups are not violent and do not involve many people. Also, elections frequently follow the coups. In spite of these events, the nation remains relatively stable.

Three important traditions hold the Thais together as a nation: their ancient reverence for their king as a living symbol of unity, their adherence to the Buddhist faith and its influence on everyday conduct, and their name and what it means—Thailand, land of the free.

Chapter 5

WATS, SPIRIT HOUSES, MOSQUES, AND CHURCHES

Wherever you go in Thailand, you are sure to see men in long robes of yellow-orange, ochre, or brown. Their heads and eyebrows are shaven clean, they are barefoot or wearing simple sandals, and often they are carrying small bowls. They may be walking, or perhaps they are riding bicycles. More often than not, they appear to be young men in their twenties.

These are *bhikkus*, Buddhist monks. To understand Thailand even a little bit, it is necessary to know something about Buddhism. About 95 percent of Thais are Buddhists, and their religion is deeply rooted in their culture, life-styles, and attitudes.

An Indian prince named Siddhartha Gautama founded Buddhism more than five hundred years before the birth of Jesus Christ. Before that, the major religion in India was Brahmanism, a branch of the Hindu religion. Early Buddhists reacted against the Brahman emphasis on caste and on sacrifice. The caste system taught that each person was born into a certain class, from which it was impossible to escape. The Brahmans were of the highest and most privileged class.

Opposite page: Buddhist monks on a busy Bangkok street

Buddhism spread over much of Asia and became the major religion in many countries. There are two main branches: *Hinayana* (lesser vehicle) and *Mahayana* (greater vehicle). Hinayana is also called Theravada, meaning "the elders." It is the older of the two branches and is the one most Thais practice.

HINAYANA BUDDHISM

Hinayana is a simpler form of worship than Mahayana and, as practiced in Thailand, it has fewer rules and ceremonies. Thai Buddhism teaches gentleness, tolerance, and love. It emphasizes disciplined meditation as the means to achieve self-control, unselfishness, knowledge, and enlightenment. It also teaches that each person lives several lives, and the condition into which a person is born depends on what kind of a life he or she lived in previous incarnations.

Everything depends on one's *karma*. Westerners sometimes translate that word as "fate," but this is not very accurate. Karma has to do with laws of cause and effect. Unhappiness comes from acting out of selfishness and greed, while unselfish acts result in happiness. The Buddhist philosophy teaches that nothing in this life is permanent, and that people therefore should not try to achieve happiness through acquiring possessions.

Buddhism is the official religion in Thailand, and all major Buddhist holy days are national holidays. The constitution of Thailand requires that the king be a Buddhist, but part of the official royal title is "Upholder of All Religions." The government contributes funds for religious education in all religions. It also allocates money for the upkeep and restoration of mosques and churches as well as of Buddhist monasteries.

SPIRIT WORSHIP

The oldest religion we know about in this part of the world is animism. This is a belief that spirits inhabit nearly everything— trees, animals, and even forces of nature such as the wind. Especially out in the country, it is believed that there are more spirits than there are people, and some of them are mean. They tease people and make them behave in strange ways. To placate these spirits, in case they are mischievous or destructive, spirit houses are built for them to live in and gifts are brought to them. If they can be kept happy in their own homes, perhaps they will stay there and leave people alone!

Foreigners visiting Thailand notice that in front of nearly every Thai residence is a small, dollhouse-like structure. It is usually overflowing with flowers, and there may also be pieces of fruit and an incense stick or two. In front of most public buildings are larger, quite beautiful shrines adorned with floral offerings brought by many people who hope the spirits will bring them good luck. These are the Thai spirit houses, called *san phra phum*.

People praying before the Brahman shrine near Bangkok's Erawan Hotel

BRAHMANISM

Another religious tradition that has survived in Thailand is Hindu Brahmanism. There are about four thousand Brahman families in the country. Many important occasions are celebrated with Brahman rituals and ceremonies. Brahman priests preside over traditional weddings and funerals, and they are called upon to say blessings over various agricultural activities. When Thai kings are crowned, they are given the names of Hindu gods. Brahmanism was traditionally associated with the monarchy, since the Brahmans were the highest caste in Hindu society. Thus a number of rules and rituals of the royal court are Hindu and Brahman in origin.

One of the best-known Brahman shrines stands in front of a modern, Western-style hotel in Bangkok called the Erawan. While this hotel was under construction there were a number of unexplainable accidents, and several workers were hurt. The

Left: An herbal medicine shop in northeast Thailand. Right: A vendor of religious objects

owners of the hotel built this large shrine to appease Brahma. It has gained such a wide reputation for bringing good luck that crowds come here to bring flowers and other gifts. It became necessary to build a special courtyard around the shrine and to assign policemen to direct the traffic.

Many Thais also hold to a number of other ancient beliefs, such as astrology, omens, and the power of wearing charms to ward off evil. Religious tattoos are believed to carry particularly strong protective powers. People consult astrologers before deciding on dates for weddings, trips, and other important events.

Though Buddhism is the official religion, it is a tolerant faith; it does not teach that other religions are wrong or bad. For this reason, many remnants of earlier beliefs are woven into everyday life and customs in Thailand. Thais see nothing strange about integrating these various ancient beliefs into their own personal philosophies.

The Buddha in the bot of Wat Chedi Luang in Chiang Mai

WHAT'S IN A WAT?

As mentioned earlier, the wat, or monastery, is the community center of a village. In some cases, a wat may be only a chapel, but in most instances it is a walled compound with a number of different buildings separated by paths and tree-shaded areas.

Buildings for worship, housing one or more statues of Buddha, are called *bots* and *viharns*. The main chapel, the bot, is high-ceilinged and houses the temple's most important statue of Buddha. The roof has usually two or three sharply pointed levels with richly decorated gables. The bot is used for the most important ceremonies. The viharn, used for meetings, meditation, and sermons, is usually built more simply than the bot.

The corncob-shaped prang *and the spired* chedi *are sacred structures seen in temple complexes throughout Thailand. Those shown here surround the Temple of the Emerald Buddha in Bangkok.*

A third sacred building is called a *stupa*. It is a building topped with a spire, built in honor of Buddha or a Buddhist saint. One type of stupa, with a sharply pointed spire rising above a bell-shaped dome set on a drumlike base, is called a *chedi*. Originally a chedi was a shrine containing relics of the Buddha. But now it has become a general symbol of Buddhism, like the Christian cross.

Another type of stupa is called a *prang*. It is much more massive and is shaped like a corncob, with a thick column that rises to an almost rounded top.

The bot, viharn, and chedi are always placed in a harmonious relationship to one another. Other buildings are often added to the wat in a random fashion—shrines, a library for sacred books, a belfry, a dormitory for pilgrims, and several small pavilions.

Most of Thailand's art and architecture has been shaped and developed by Buddhism, and the wats are especially impressive. Visitors to Thailand are fascinated by these beautiful compounds. Almost all wats are open to the public most or all of the time. People entering temples are expected to remove their shoes. Proper clothing for a house of worship is also expected.

BUDDHIST MONKS

Many Buddhist monks seen on the streets of Thailand appear to be very young. That is because it is traditional for a young Thai male to enter the monastery for a short time after he is twenty years old. The usual period is three months. The young monks spend this time studying the religion, practicing meditation, and clearing the mind of material matters. Like the permanent monks, they wear saffron robes and shave their heads and eyebrows.

All monks, whether temporary or permanent, go out in the early morning carrying a small bowl, called an alms bowl. They call on families who give them food for breakfast. Those who donate food are earning Buddhist merit for their generosity.

Buddhism teaches that parents of the young monks also earn merit because of their sons' entry into the monkhood. The boys undertake the discipline as gifts of gratitude to their parents.

The traditional time for young men to be ordained as monks is in July, at the beginning of the rainy season. Anyone who works for the government, armed services, or a large private company may take four months' leave with pay to go to a monastery.

A man can go into the temporary monkhood more than once if he wishes. Older men who no longer have any families to support often spend their last years as monks.

Young students of Buddhism at Wat Po Temple

A Buddhist monk has literally hundreds of rules he should obey. He must not steal, lie, kill any living creature (including insects), or indulge in idle talk, sex, intoxicating drink, or frivolous amusements. The only possessions he is allowed to have are his robes, alms bowl, and a very few personal items such as a toothbrush. He is allowed only two meals a day, both of them before 11:00 A.M.

Until fairly recently, almost every young Buddhist male hoped to have the experience of being a monk. In fact, many young women would not be willing to marry a man who had not been a monk, believing that this was a necessary part of becoming an adult. Today, especially among the well-educated men who live in the city, the custom has declined. Many now believe that one can be a perfectly good Buddhist without having been a monk.

Buddhist women taking part in a three-day prayer retreat

Before his death, Gautama established a religious order for Buddhist females, but there are few active female orders in Thailand today. Buddhist women earn merit by attending services, preparing and giving food to the monks, and helping take care of the temples. In fact, women are much more involved in these activities than are men.

The headquarters of the World Fellowship of Buddhists is in Thailand, and Thai monks travel to a number of foreign countries as missionaries.

MINORITY RELIGIONS

The largest religious minority in Thailand is Islam. Its members are followers of Muhammad and are known as Muslims. Islam is particularly strong in the south of Thailand, among people of Malay descent. As supporter of all religions, the king presides over the annual ceremonies to celebrate Muhammad's birthday.

The religion of Islam requires every able-bodied Muslim to make a pilgrimage to Mecca, called a *haj*, at least once in his or her lifetime. In the same way that Buddhist men are given a paid leave of absence from their jobs to perform their obligations as monks, it is the custom to grant a Muslim employee a leave of four months to make a *haj*.

Confucianism and ancestor worship are part of the Thai religious tradition, especially among the Chinese Thais—usually in conjunction with the practice of Buddhism.

Some Chinese Thais are followers of Mahayana Buddhism. The Mahayana monks wear Chinese-style jackets and trousers and are strict vegetarians. There are also a number of Vietnamese who are Mahayanas, but they do not follow quite such strict rules as their Chinese counterparts.

There are a few thousand Hindus and Sikhs, most of whom are of Indian descent. Both Hindus and Buddhists worship at certain Brahman shrines. There is a Hindu school, where the languages of Hindi and Sanskrit are taught along with the normal Thai courses.

European Christian missionaries were permitted to come into Thailand as early as the seventeenth century. Because of the Buddhist tradition of tolerance, there was little objection to this teaching of another religion. But since Christianity is a religion that expects its followers to give up such beliefs as spirit worship, it is not very compatible with traditional Thai philosophy. There are some Catholics, Presbyterians, Baptists, and Seventh-Day Adventists, but not very many. Most Christians in Thailand are immigrants from China.

On the other hand, there are many Christian-affiliated schools and hospitals. Western medicine and surgery were introduced to Thailand by Christian missionaries. King Mongkut is reputed to have said to his Christian friends, "What you teach us to *do* is admirable, but what you teach us to *believe* is foolish."

Chapter 6

RICE PADDIES,
SILKWORMS,
AND ELEPHANTS

Thailand is the only nation in Asia that not only produces enough food for its own people but also has surplus food to export. In fact, it is one of the largest food exporters in the world.

The majority of Thailand's people make a living in one way or another from the land. There are three interesting and traditional kinds of work done in the country's rural areas; all of them are very different from work done in Western countries. Let's take a look at rice growing in the central plains, silkworm raising in the northeast, and lumbering in the northern mountains.

RICE AND THE SEASONS

For the rice growers of Thailand's central plains, the entire year's activities are determined by the rice-growing cycles — the seasons of planting, growing, and harvesting. The school calendar follows these cycles, and most important holidays and celebrations fit into the rhythms of the rice fields.

Left: Planting rice. Right: Water buffalo pulling a plow

Each year in April or May, the king officially opens the planting season by presiding over the Royal Plowing Ceremony in Bangkok. This is the hottest time of year, and schoolchildren are on vacation.

Everyone in the villages, including the older children, work together. First they plow the fields, then they irrigate them with water from the streams or canals, and finally they set out young rice seedlings. In many villages, water buffalo are used to pull the plows. However, machinery is seen more and more and eventually may replace the buffalo.

Everyone who is able is involved in this important work. While it is going on, the older people of the village take care of the small children and prepare meals.

The celebration of Buddha's birthday, called Visakha Puja, comes during this time of year. This is the most important holiday of the year, not only in Thailand but also in many other Buddhist

Monsoon clouds over Laos, as seen across the Mekong River from Thailand

countries. In the evening, after the day's work in the fields is completed, each person lights three incense sticks and a candle or torch and carries them, along with some flowers, in a parade that proceeds three times around the temple chapel.

Soon after the planting is finished come the monsoons, the heavy rains that flood all the fields. It rains every day for three or four months, then stops as suddenly as it began. This rainy season is also the Buddhist holy season, sometimes called Buddhist Lent. The monks are in retreat during this period and use the time for meditation and study.

This is also the usual time for ordination of young men who are entering the monastery temporarily. The ordination ceremony has a significance beyond its religious importance: it is a rite of passage into adulthood. Many people still believe that a man who has not been a monk cannot be considered mature.

The ordination ceremony is an occasion for the whole village to celebrate, because ordination is considered one of the four most important celebrations in a man's life. The other three are the birth ceremony, marriage, and cremation.

The candidate for ordination, called the *nak*, shaves his head and eyebrows and puts on a long white robe. He leads everyone in a parade three times around the temple, carrying the traditional threesome—a flower, an incense stick, and a candle. This is not a solemn procession, but a joyous one. Children join in, drums are beaten, and the people dance along. Then the nak takes his oath.

The end of the holy season marks the time for another celebration, called Thot Kathin. This is a time for entertainment, homecoming, and merit-making. Movies, dancing, and music are presented at a village festival. People who have gone away to the city for employment come back to visit the village. Merit-making is accomplished by presenting new robes to the monks. Money, books about Buddhism, and other objects may also be given.

As the rice is ripening in the fields, the farmers must be vigilant to keep birds and mice from eating the young grain. It is also a prime time of the year for fishing in the streams and canals that crisscross the paddies.

Early in November another holiday provides an opportunity for fun and entertainment, called Loi Krathong. The *krathong* is a lotus-shaped basket, the size of a small saucer, made of banana leaves. *Loi* means "to float." Once again people gather together a candle, three incense sticks, and some flowers, and place them in the krathongs. Some coins may be added, too. Everyone gathers at the side of a stream or other body of water, or gets into a boat. After dark they light the candles and incense, make wishes, and set the krathongs afloat. The belief is that water spirits will carry

Left: A child ready to set a Loi Krathong basket afloat. Right: People celebrate Songkran, or Thai New Year, by throwing water at one another.

away all the past year's sins and wipe the slate clean for the coming year. It is a beautiful ceremony, with thousands of flickering lights floating on waterways under the moonlit sky.

Soon after Loi Krathong comes harvest time. Once again, children have a vacation from school so that they can help with the work. The villagers work together in groups, going from farm to farm to cut the rice down with sickles and lay it out to dry. Each family whose farm is being tended furnishes one meal for all the workers at noon and another after the day's work is done.

The harvest is finished in January or February, except in the extreme south of Thailand, where it may be later.

The beginning of the Thai New Year, in April, is marked by another festival, Songkran. This holiday comes at the hottest season of the year, and one of the ways people celebrate it is to throw water at each other all day. Soon after Songkran, the cycle of rice culture begins again.

THAI SILK

Thai silk is famous throughout the world. Between 300,000 and 400,000 Thai families work in sericulture, the production of silkworms and silk fiber. Silk has been produced in Asia for thousands of years. Some authorities say the industry is as much as six thousand years old. It probably started in China, where it was a jealously kept secret for many centuries. Anyone who let the secret out to foreigners received the death penalty.

The parent of the silkworms is an adult female moth that lives as an adult for only about five days. During that short life span, the moth lays from 350 to 600 eggs—eggs so tiny that some 30,000 of them weigh only about an ounce (twenty-eight grams).

When the silkworms hatch, they are called larvae. They live in this stage for only about four weeks, and they spend just about all of that time eating.

When this stage of life is completed, the larvae begin to spin a cocoon, a tight little nest whose fiber can be made into fine thread. There is only one food that gives these larvae the proper nutrition to produce silk fibers: the leaves of mulberry trees.

Most of the Thai sericulture is carried on in the northeastern region of the country, by individual farm families. Women and children harvest the cocoons and drop them into boiling water. This accomplishes two things. It kills the insect and it loosens the soft outer fibers. Then the raw silk threads can be wound onto wooden bobbins.

Silk brokers buy the coils of raw silk thread and sell them to textile manufacturers in Bangkok. There the fibers are dyed, taken out into the bright sunlight to dry, and then reeled once more onto bobbins, spun, and woven.

Left: Inspecting a mulberry bush
Below: Silk cocoons
Bottom left: Dyeing silk threads
Bottom right: Bolts of Thai silk cloth

Jim Thompson's home in Bangkok can be visited by the public.

Some of the cloth is printed with beautiful, intricate patterns of peacocks, tigers, flowers, and other designs in a variety of brilliant colors. The process is called silk-screen printing. Skilled workers place fine screens over the shiny cloth, which has been spread out on long tables. Using one color at a time, they squeeze the dye through the screens until as many as seven colors have been used.

Thais give credit for the modern development of their silk industry to an American man by the name of Jim Thompson, who went to live in Thailand in the 1940s.

Thompson persuaded silk weavers to use bright, colorfast chemical dyes from Germany and Switzerland instead of the vegetable dyes they had traditionally used. He also pioneered in exporting Thai silk.

The story of Jim Thompson is a local legend—and an unsolved mystery. He loved Thailand and appreciated the skill and craftsmanship of native artisans. As a hobby he collected many lovely antiques and works of art. One day while on a short vacation in a mountain area of neighboring Malaysia, he went out for a walk and never returned. No one ever found out what happened to him.

A girl carving designs into teakwood

LUMBERING IN THAILAND

Northern Thailand is an area with dense forests of teak trees. Teak is an extremely valuable and durable wood. It is used for shipbuilding and furniture manufacture, and it has been an important trade product for Thailand for centuries.

Here in the forestland is a unique school, known as the Center for Training Baby Elephants. Long used in Southeast Asia as cavalry in wartime and as beasts of burden in peacetime, elephants are particularly valuable in the lumber industry. They can climb steep slopes that would be very difficult, if not impossible, for motorized vehicles to manage. They can pick up huge logs with their tusks and carry them down to the riverfront to be floated to the mills.

Elephants are trained to pick up logs with their tusks.

The training center is a pleasant compound. Homes for the staff are built of teak and bamboo; a small stream is spanned by a bamboo bridge; there are training cages for the elephants, a reviewing grandstand, and practice grounds.

Trainers and veterinarians are in charge. The center is concerned with breeding elephants and protecting the young ones from their natural enemies, as well as with teaching them tasks.

The elephant trainers are called *mahouts*. Two of them are permanently assigned to each elephant calf; it is their responsibility from that time on. One mahout teaches the elephant to carry him on its back. The other trains the animal to get used to the leg chains, harnesses, and other lumbering equipment.

The first lesson the elephant learns is to lift one front leg and lower its head so that the "neck mahout" can climb on its back. Then it is given obedience training. It is taught to pick up objects with its trunk and present them to its master. It learns that certain leg pressures indicate the direction in which it should walk.

Elephants and their mahouts at the Center for Training Baby Elephants

Finally, training begins for the actual tasks the elephant will be performing for all its working days. It learns to pick up logs— small ones at first—and balance them on its tusks. The trainers are very careful not to overload the tusks, as damage to the tusks affects the elephant's eyes.

The training period is very long and intensive. The young calves are kept at the center until they are ten years old, and they are trained for six hours every morning, except for a three-month holiday during the dry, hot season. After this they are put to work, but their loads are restricted until they are fully grown.

The Center for Training Baby Elephants is a fascinating place to visit. The animals are put through their paces every day, and outsiders make appointments to come and watch them practice. Some of the demonstrations include going through the rituals of ancient battles, walking over a dozen men lying flat on the ground without touching them, and going through certain steps and motions like dancers on a chorus line.

Left: Fishing boats coming in with their catches
Right: Durian fruits

OTHER AGRICULTURE

While rice is the most important agricultural product of Thailand, many other foods are produced in enough quantity for export. Tapioca is almost as important in bringing revenues into the country as is rice. In at least one recent year, sales income from tapioca was greater than from rice.

When sugar prices skyrocketed all over the world in the 1970s, a boom in the production and processing of cane sugar started in Thailand. Other important agricultural products are maize, mushrooms, orchids, and natural rubber.

Dozens of tropical fruits flourish in the humid climate, especially in the south of Thailand. Some of them are unfamiliar to most Americans, such as durians, rambutans, tamarinds, palm fruits, and pomelos. Others are less strange: oranges, strawberries, pineapples, and more than twenty varieties of banana.

Thailand ranks among the world's top dozen marine fishing nations. In Asia, only Japan and China have larger catches. Frozen shrimp is a very important Thai export.

A steel mill near Bangkok

MANUFACTURING AND MINING

At present, less than one worker in ten is employed in manufacturing in Thailand. Textile manufacturing and microchip assembly are the fastest growing industries. Other manufacturing is also increasing, and the country is much less dependent on imports for manufactured goods than it used to be.

Thailand's mines produce rubies and sapphires, tin, bauxite, and other minerals used in industry. Natural gas and oil deposits have been found in the north, the northeast, and the Gulf of Thailand, but they have not been extensively tapped as yet.

TOURISM

Tourism is becoming the most important factor in Thailand's economy, and many modern resort and convention facilities have been built. The areas that send the most tourists to Thailand are, in order: Malaysia, Japan, Great Britian (including Hong Kong), Singapore, the United States, the Middle East, Germany, India, Australia, China, and Taiwan.

Chapter 7

GROWING UP IN THAILAND

Children who grow up in the villages of Thailand are surrounded by relatives and neighbors. Often they live in the same house or compound with their grandparents and some of their aunts, uncles, and cousins, as well as with their parents and brothers and sisters. The house may be small, but most of the day's activities take place outdoors in the warm sunshine.

Children are taught early to respect their elders, and the habit of deferring to older relatives, friends, and acquaintances is something that lasts throughout life. Thus, elderly people in Thailand enjoy a place of honor in the family and the community.

As young people move to the cities for employment and start their own families, it becomes less possible for the extended family to stay together, but it is still accepted as an important part of the Thai way of life. Frequent visits to the home village are made, especially for harvest season and for important holidays.

A TYPICAL DAY IN A VILLAGE

Shortly before sunrise, the woman of the house gets up and starts preparing breakfast over a charcoal fire. She cooks more than enough for her family's needs, so that she will have something ready to give the monks when they make their rounds with their alms bowls. The rest of the family gets a little extra sleep, lying on their sleeping mats on the floor.

When the older children get up, they go to feed the family's livestock and chickens, while the father does a few other chores.

Bathing is done in the stream, canal, or lake. Standards of personal hygiene are high in Thailand; most people bathe at least twice a day. After everyone is washed and dressed and has completed the morning tasks, the family sits down on the floor to eat together. Then the children take off to school, the men to the fields. The mother may go to market.

All the family members are usually at home by five. They eat a leisurely supper and socialize together for a while. The children may go out later to listen to a local storyteller entertaining a group. Except when festivals are being celebrated, the whole family goes to bed early.

The workday is longer and harder during planting and harvesting, but during much of the year the villagers enjoy a fairly relaxed life-style.

Teenagers enjoy doing many of the activities popular in other parts of the world—swimming in the rivers, going to a beach, watching movies, going to village fairs, cockfights, and boxing matches. Traveling movies and video shows also play in villages. In addition, there are many burlesque folk-drama troupes, called *likee*, that travel from village to village.

THE VILLAGE APPEARANCE

The population of most rural villages in Thailand ranges from five hundred to two thousand inhabitants. There are three types

A typical farm cottage in rural Thailand

of villages. One is a settlement that is stretched out along a canal, river, or highway. Another is a cluster of houses in a grove of trees. A third type of village is a collection of somewhat isolated farmhouses, with a wat nearby where people meet for religious celebrations or to conduct village business. In rural Thailand, a village without a wat is not considered "civilized."

Near each individual home or family compound is a small wooden structure on stilts, a storehouse for grain. Large earthenware jars are here and there; their purpose is to catch rainwater for drinking. Water for other purposes, such as washing and cooking, comes from canals, rivers, or wells. The village wat, spirit house, store, and school are usually found in the center of the settlement.

A primary school for children in an Akha tribal village

SCHOOLS

Education is compulsory through the sixth grade, and more than 99 percent of primary-age children are enrolled in school. The government runs village schools, and there are also quite a few private secondary schools, especially in the larger towns and cities. Some Chinese families send their children to schools that teach the Chinese language as well as Thai.

American children would be surprised at the behavior of Thai children in school. Because they are trained to respect their elders, they are not quick to ask questions or volunteer answers. The teacher does most of the talking, and when he or she asks for a response, the children drop their eyes in the hope that they will not be called on.

Left: A takraw tournament. Right: Kites for sale

Most teaching in the villages used to be done by monks, in the wats, but today public schools provide general education. The monks are still important influences in moral and spiritual training, and they provide religious instruction at temple schools.

Schools sponsor extracurricular activities, such as team sports and scouting. One popular game is called *takraw*. It is a combination of volleyball and soccer, with the ball propelled over a net by the feet and head. In another kind of *takraw*, players use their feet and head to get a ball through a suspended hoop. During the windy seasons, children and adults like to fly kites, both for individual pleasure and in competition.

After school, children come home to help with the family chores and do their homework. They are given heavier work loads as they get older, and by the time they are in their middle teens they have taken on nearly as much responsibility as adults have.

Chulalongkorn University in Bangkok

There are more than a dozen universities in Thailand and about three times as many teachers' colleges. Competition is stiff to get into some of the better universities. Because of this, the government has established two universities for the large number of young people who want higher education but have not been accepted in the other colleges and universities. Entrance examinations are not required in these two institutions.

Many Thai students go on to postgraduate study, either in Thailand or in Europe or the United States. Some who come to America find it difficult at first to join in classroom discussions along with their American classmates—especially when there are other Thai students in the class who might think they are being too aggressive. This shyness soon wears off, though.

Other educational programs include agricultural and technical schools, mobile vocational schools that go out to rural areas, adult retraining programs, and radio and television instruction.

A young couple on their wedding day receive the blessings of local monks.

MARRIAGE

Although a few marriages are still arranged, most young men and women in Thailand choose their own mates. It is traditional for the groom to make a formal proposal and to seek the approval of the bride's family. Usually an astrologer will be consulted to see whether or not the couple will be compatible.

The day of a wedding in a village starts with a presentation of food and small gifts by the bride and groom to the local monks, who then bless the couple and their home. The ceremony is a simple one: the village elders watch while the couple's wrists are tied together to symbolize the union, then a party starts. In some sections, the guests pour fragrant water over the hands or heads of the couple as a blessing.

Left: A Thai family meal. Right: Thailand offers an amazing variety of fresh produce.

THAI FOOD

Like the French in Europe, the Thai are proud of their cuisine. Thai food is excellent, plentiful, and full of variety. This is not a land of scarcity. For the most part the lines inscribed on the pillar in Sukhothai nearly seven hundred years ago are still true; there are still fish in the waters and rice in the fields. There are also all those wonderful local fruits and a distinctive tradition of cooking.

Many spices and herbs are used in Thai food. Hot peppers, garlic, and coriander are the most popular seasonings. Ginger, onions, and curries are used liberally. People who like only bland food would have a hard time at a typical Thai table. A contrast to the hotly seasoned meat and fish dishes is provided by steamed rice or mild noodle dishes, sweet desserts, and fruits.

Typical desserts are sticky rice baked with coconut sauce or fruit, banana fritters or banana in coconut milk, and custards. A delicious sweetmeat, called *kanom krok*, is made of a mixture of shredded coconut, coconut milk, and various other ingredients. The mixture is poured into shallow pans and cooked to crispness over an open fire. Other confections called *look-chob* are shaped and decorated to look like miniature fruits and vegetables. They are coated with gelatin to give them a gloss, and the flavor is something like marzipan.

Thais ordinarily eat with a fork and a spoon, not with chopsticks. This is because most of their foods are either soupy or quite soft.

The cuisine varies a bit in the different regions of the country. Meals in the north are somewhat milder than in the central plains; northeastern food is fiery hot. Seafoods are most common in the south, and the Muslim communities of the deep south are partial to all kinds of curries.

Party meals in Thailand are usually as attractive to the eye as to the taste buds. Thai cooks are skillful at sculpting fruits and vegetables into the shapes of flowers, vases, bowls, and other objects. Mothers teach their daughters this skill.

Because Bangkok is a cosmopolitan city and a commercial crossroads, it has numerous restaurants that serve the authentic foods of many foreign countries and regions. Among them are Mexican, American, Italian, French, German, Scandinavian, Swiss, Hungarian, Austrian, Lebanese, Chinese, Japanese, Korean, Vietnamese, Laotian, Filipino, Burmese, Indonesian, and Indian. Western foods like hot dogs, hamburgers, doughnuts, and pizza have become popular in recent years with many of Bangkok's young people.

Left: Thai women construction workers. Above: Thai villagers, in modern dress, prepare to go shopping on a motorcycle.

TRADITIONAL CLOTHING

Everyday clothing worn by young people living in towns and cities is similar to that worn by people of their age in the Western world—shirts or T-shirts and jeans for casual wear; loose, cool shirts and slacks or blouses and skirts for more serious occasions.

For formal parties, women blossom forth in gorgeous silk dresses or long skirts and blouses, and men dress in suits. However, some men like to dress in the style of clothes once worn by members of the royal court. This consists of a large, loose lower garment called a *phanung* and a high-collared cotton jacket.

For many centuries before modern times, women of Thailand wore a *paa sin*, a skirt fashioned from a tube of material about 2 yards (1.8 meters) wide and long enough to reach from the waist to the floor. The wearer would fold the tube over in the front to fit her measurements, then tuck the top into a gold or silver belt. A blouse and a *sabai* completed the outfit. A sabai is a silk shawl draped over the left shoulder. Many modern formal dresses and suits worn by city women are made of silk and are modified versions of the traditional costume.

When working in the rice paddies or selling goods from boats, women wear an attractive straw hat that is ingeniously designed for maximum coolness—there is a small frame that rests on the head, while the high-crowned, broad-brimmed hat is held above the frame. Thus the hat serves as a small sunshade; it does not rest directly on the head.

Farmers generally wear a shirt and shorts, plus a *phakhaoma*. This is a strip of cloth that is loosely tied around the waist and can be used alternately as a turban, a loincloth while bathing, a cradle, a rope, a belt, or a towel.

Village women wear a *phasin*, a sort of sarong, and a blouse. Children wear uniforms to school.

HILL TRIBES OF THE NORTH

In the remote mountains of northern Thailand live various. people known as the hill tribes. They continue to practice life-styles that have been handed down from generation to generation and that are quite different from those of the other Thais. The major tribal groupings are the Karen, Hmong, Mien, Akha, Lisu, and Lahu. The Karen are the most numerous. Each group has its own language, style of dress, and traditional celebrations. Many of the older people do not speak the Thai language.

Three factors are at work to bring about profound changes in the hill villages: government schools, roads, and radios.

Most of the children are now enrolled in government schools, where they learn the Thai language. Some of the elders approve of this and are anxious for young people to be educated. Others are afraid that outsiders teaching in the villages will steer the children away from traditional tribal values.

*A girl in a mountain village walks her beasts
to the tune of her transistor radio.*

Roads are being built into the hill villages, making it easier for outsiders to come in and for the villagers to travel outside. This, too, is seen as a mixed blessing. On the one hand, the roads make it easier to transport farm products and handicrafts to markets. On the other hand, hill people cherish their privacy and do not appreciate being intruded upon by curious strangers.

Radios and cassette recorders are popular among the tribal people. There are radios in almost every village, informing the residents about what is going on in the world, and tribal radio stations broadcast programs of local interest. Traditional songs and legends are recorded in the villages and sent to the stations to be aired.

Gradually, these and other modernizing influences draw the tribal people toward the mainstream of Thai culture. But as yet there are many distinctive habits and customs that make each tribal group unique.

A few groups have adopted the practices of Islam, Buddhism, or Christianity, but ancient animism is the most prevailing belief.

Typical clothing varies from one tribal group to another. Hmong men and women are recognized by their huge black

Left: A black-turbaned Hmong woman. Right: An Akha woman in her headdress

turbans and chunky silver jewelry. Mien women wear dark blue skirts decorated with red and white bands of embroidery. Most of the women are skilled in fine needlework, and they cover jackets, handbags, and even baby clothing with intricate embroidery and appliqués.

Akha women wear hand-embroidered jackets and knee-length skirts. The most distinctive part of their costume is the hat, or headdress. Shaped like a helmet, the headpiece is completely covered with adornments of silver, beads, and sometimes feathers.

Karen weavers are famous; their red and black clothing is simple in design but made of beautiful homespun cotton cloth and decorated with braid and stitching.

Handwoven blouses worn by Lisu girls are brightly striped; they wear sashes with long tassels and use silver to create earrings, neck collars, rings, and bracelets.

Left: Chopping wood in the northern forest. Right: Young married women of the Karen tribe

In general, the young people nearing marriageable age wear the most colorful clothing. But American blue jeans and T-shirts have found their way even into these remote Asian mountains, and it is likely that before long the colorful and exotic costumes of Thailand's hill tribes will be seen only on special holidays.

The ethnic backgrounds of the hill people include strains from China, Burma, Laos, and Tibet. Some tribes frown on marriages outside the tribe, and it is not uncommon for a man to have more than one wife.

The hill people make their living in a variety of ways. Most of them are farmers, but they also get much of their food by hunting, fishing, and gathering food from the jungle. Many of them are also highly talented artisans, and much of the handicrafts for which Thailand is famous come from this section of the country. Children are taught at an early age the skills and crafts practiced by their parents or other older members of their tribe.

Wood carvers in Bangkok

HANDICRAFTS

Chiang Mai is the crafts capital of Thailand. People from the hill settlements bring their wares here for sale. Many artisans make their homes in Chiang Mai. Tourists come here from other parts of Thailand, as well as from foreign countries, to watch the craftspeople at work and to buy their products. Each craft has its own section of the city. There is a silversmith's street, a lacquerware road, and so on. Umbrellas and handwoven silk are made in nearby villages.

Wood carving is one of the more important crafts of Chiang Mai. About two hundred children here spend part of each day carving blocks of teakwood into bowls, trays, furniture, and figures. Elephants are especially popular. Hand-carved elephant

Left: A silversmith in Chiang Mai. Right: Making lacquerware boxes

figures range in size from around an inch (twenty-five millimeters) in height to almost life-size. The children work from patterns drawn by a designer.

Silversmiths make jewelry and hammer out thin bowls. A piece of silver is placed over a wooden form and pounded. Intricate designs, sometimes of scenes from Buddhist literature, are beaten into the metal.

Many lovely objects are made from lacquerware—trays, plates, bowls, and boxes, among others. The most typical lacquerware is black and gold, but brightly colored objects in orange, green, and yellow are also made. First the artist makes a framework of bamboo strips, sometimes even elephant hair is used. Many layers of lacquer are then applied. Each layer is dried and polished before the next is added.

Girl painting designs on a paper and bamboo umbrella

Close to the city is a small village where young men and women are hard at work making umbrellas (actually sunshades) from paper and bamboo. The men cut and trim cane stems, and the women make umbrella frames out of strips of bamboo. The frames are covered with a sheet of thin, locally manufactured paper, then hand painted with cheerful designs. Most of this is done in homes that double as shops. The rattle of looms can be heard in the next village, where young girls are weaving silk thread into lengths of shiny, brilliant cloth. Another village specializes in cotton. Seamstresses and tailors can transform the cloth into made-to-order clothing with unbelievable speed.

Other prized local products are baskets, mobiles woven of basketwork, bronze tableware and bells, and lovely, green-hued celadon pottery.

Chapter 8

GLITTERING TEMPLES, GRACEFUL DANCERS

The walls of Thailand's hundreds of temples and palaces gleam and glitter in the long months of brilliant sunshine. Light reflects from shiny bits of glass and tile, lacquer, precious stones, and gilt paint. Every square inch of the surface appears to have some part in the intricate designs.

Traditional art in Thailand pulsates with color and complex detail. The arts of both India and China have had an influence. These ancient cultures developed art forms that added detail on detail, in their buildings, paintings, sculpture, furniture, and other works of art.

Add to these influences the scenes that ancient artists saw around them, the colors of nature in the bright, hot climate of Southeast Asia; the flashy hues of native flowers, and the gaudy plumage of tropical birds, the green of the forests and fertile fields, and the blue of the waters and clear skies. Yes, the work of Thailand's early artists was elaborate and fanciful—but so was nature, as they saw it.

Opposite page: Teakwood doors on a temple in Chiang Mai

A glittering mural in the Temple of the Emerald Buddha compound

Nature supplied the colors, and the complex world of religion furnished the subject matter. Figures of Buddha, episodes from his life, Hindu gods, spirit figures, and mythical animals are worked into designs along with flowers and trees, animals, fish, and birds. They march along the walls of structures, strut across murals, and are worked into carvings and inlays in marvelous array.

The art of the Sukhothai period (1238-1350) was less intricate than that created in Thailand later on. Art experts have acclaimed the simple, dignified statues of Buddha carved during the earlier period as some of the finest religious art ever created. During succeeding centuries it became fashionable to add more and more ornamentation.

ARCHITECTURE

Traditional Thai architecture has been best expressed in temples, which seem to soar toward the sky. Each structure has

*Religious symbols
on the roof of
a Thai temple*

several tiers of roofs that sweep steeply upward in a slightly
concave line. This shape, so pleasing to the eye, is said to have
been copied from the natural look of an ordinary thatched roof
that has been soaked and weighted down with rain.

At the ends of the roof ridges are ornaments called *chawfas*.
Their unusual shape may have been copied from that of animal
horns, but they look like slim flames licking at the gables.

Sacred serpents carved of wood are sometimes added to the
gables, their bodies slithering and their tails pointing up. All these
details add to the impression that the whole building is stretching
toward the heavens.

The Hindu god Vishnu and a creature called the Garuda are
symbols of Thai kings and are used widely in architectural
decoration. The Temple of the Emerald Buddha, in Bangkok, is
adorned with long rows of gleaming, gilt Garudas at the base of
the exterior.

Legendary Garudas guard the Temple of the Emerald Buddha.

Mythology says that the Garuda is half man, half bird, and is the creature on which the god Vishnu rides. It has the head, beak, and wings of an eagle, atop the body of a man—a combination that gives it a fierce appearance. The Garuda eats serpents and is sometimes depicted with a serpent in each hand. It can fly as fast as a flash of lightning.

Decorations on temples and palaces are made of many kinds of materials. There are carvings of stone and wood, mosaics of porcelain and glass. Lacquerwork, gilt, mother-of-pearl inlay, and gold leaf add to the glitter.

PAINTING AND SCULPTURE

Classical Thai painting was used almost exclusively in three ways—to create murals for temples and palaces, to illustrate palm-leaf books, and to decorate the bookcases in which these texts were kept. Subjects included demons, gods riding in chariots, members of royalty, and stylized animals.

Wat Po Temple is also known as the Temple of the Thousand Buddhas.

In early days the pigments used were subdued and did not withstand the ravages of time very well. Richer and longer-lasting colors were imported from China in the eighteenth century, and chemical colors from the West were introduced about a hundred years later.

Ancient sculptors confined their work to creating images of Buddha. Several million of them have been produced in Thailand. The early style is still most typical of Thai art—a smooth, elongated figure with no muscles, bone structure, or veins showing. Buddha always has an enigmatic smile, which along with the simple figure symbolizes the ideal of serenity and enlightenment.

The Buddha is always shown in one of seven poses. The three most often seen are sitting, reclining, and walking. A huge walking Buddha was constructed in 1980 at Phuttha Monthon to commemorate more than 2,500 years of Buddhism. Thai Buddhist figures are most frequently made of stone, marble, and bronze.

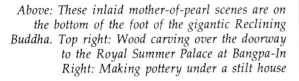

Above: These inlaid mother-of-pearl scenes are on the bottom of the foot of the gigantic Reclining Buddha. Top right: Wood carving over the doorway to the Royal Summer Palace at Bangpa-In Right: Making pottery under a stilt house

The vast teak forests of Thailand have furnished a wood that is ideal for wood carving, since it is both soft enough to cut and resistant to the appetites of termites.

Traditional wood-carving styles in Thailand contrast strikingly with the smooth and simple lines of Buddha images. Elaborate and complex carvings, filling every bit of the available space, adorn royal barges, thrones, elephant howdahs (seats for riding), doors, house lintels and braces, and furniture. Unfortunately, the art of wood carving is dying out in Thailand, except for the work being done for sale to tourists.

MODERN ART

Modern art in Thailand is a thriving activity, and is strongly supported by banks, hotels, and corporations. Many such institutions regard the work of modern artists as an expression of the changing and dynamic nature of Thai society. Five major art exhibitions are held every year, and every week two or three smaller exhibitions typically open in Bangkok.

Modern Thai art fuses international designs and colors with the traditional Thai interest in religion and nature. It is a dazzling art pursued by men and women who have inherited—and added to—the traditional Thai love of the beautiful.

OTHER ARTS

The art of making ceramics and pottery in Thailand was greatly influenced by Chinese styles. Subjects portrayed were similar to those used for murals—mythological creatures, animals, and birds.

Mother-of-pearl is popularly used for inlay work. The methods are slow and painstaking.

First the shell of a creature called *muk fai*, found only in the Gulf of Thailand, is carefully cut into hundreds of tiny, paper-thin pieces. These are sanded and glued in patterns onto wooden surfaces. Black lacquer is brushed into the spaces between the pieces of luminous shell. It takes seven coats, applied and allowed to dry for a week between coats, to build up the lacquer to the same height as that of the shell. Finally, the last coat is left to dry for two weeks, then sanded and polished to a bright and lovely luster.

PERFORMING ARTS

The dances of Thailand, or imitations of them, have been shown in many a Hollywood movie. Petite young men and women dressed in shiny costumes, faces covered with masks, headdresses pointing upward like temple spires, go through graceful but strenuous movements that are unmistakably Asian in style.

The Thai dance-drama was derived from temple rituals of India. The most formal, difficult, and traditional type is the *khon*, originally performed only in the royal palaces. Productions went on for days. Shorter versions are presented now in the National Theater in Bangkok. Training for this arduous and acrobatic dancing starts when children are as young as six years old. From the beginning each dancer is trained to take one of four roles—man, woman, demon, or monkey.

Costumes and masks are spectacular. Kohn masks are works of art. Papier-mâché is built up painstakingly over a plaster-of-Paris mold. A special thin tissue paper made from a local tree bark is used; fifteen to twenty layers are applied over a period of several days. After the mask has fully dried it is painted and decorated with lacquer, gold leaf, and jewels. The result is a very durable product; some masks on display at the National Museum are more than a hundred years old.

The dancers' costumes are sewn of rich brocade material, designed to resemble the clothing worn by gods and kings in classical murals.

Silpakorn University (the University of Fine Arts) is active in keeping the art of classical dance-drama alive. Students of music, dance, acting, and singing regularly present performances there for the public.

Left: Thai dancers performing in a restaurant. Right: The fingernail dance

A less formal dance-drama is the *lakhon*. The dancers do not wear masks, and the stories are taken from folk fables and Buddhist tales. Lakhon dancers are hired to perform near popular shrines. People who have had extraordinarily good luck pay the dancers as thanks to the spirits thought to be responsible for the fortunate events.

Folk dances, differing from one region to another, are performed by villagers at local fairs. These are very different from Thai classical dance, just as folk dancing contrasts with formal ballet in Western countries.

One very popular regional dance is the fingernail dance, which originated in the north of Thailand around Chiang Mai. This dance is frequently seen in photographs and paintings of Thai customs and entertainment. At one time, women of leisure grew unusually long fingernails to symbolize their wealth and beauty.

Musicians playing traditional Thai musical instruments

When performing the fingernail dance, young women attach long gold or bronze fingernails to their fingers to accentuate their graceful hand and finger movements.

MUSIC

Thai music, like most Asian music, sounds strange to Western ears because it is based on a different scale than the one we are accustomed to hearing.

Many native musical instruments have been invented and constructed in Thailand—stringed instruments, gongs, and a kind of xylophone. As in other arts, the music of Thailand has absorbed features from India and other Asian countries. In addition to the instruments native to Thailand, other instruments come from Java, Malaysia, and Burma.

In Thai boxing, the feet as well as the hands are used.

Western classical music was introduced to Thailand late in the nineteenth century. The royal family encouraged the establishment of a few orchestras in the 1920s, and in 1982 the Bangkok Symphony Orchestra, formed of sixty musicians from all walks of life, presented its first public concert. It has not yet achieved widespread popularity, but it may in time.

Other popular and traditional forms of entertainment are shadow plays, puppet shows, and boxing. Thai boxing does not resemble the boxing seen in other countries. Thai boxers are barefoot, and they perform with a mixture of balletic grace and ferocious intensity. The fighters use their elbows, shoulders, knees, and especially their feet for attack. The entire performance is accompanied by the music of a four-piece orchestra.

New ways and old ways meet in a Bangkok market.

Chapter 9

LOOKING TO
THE FUTURE

Thailand is a fascinating and picturesque place. But if we examine only those aspects that are strange and unusual, we miss a lot of the truth. The saffron-robed monks, the women bearing shoulder-poles filled with produce, the sampans and gaudily decorated fishing boats, the flower-filled spirit houses, the temples—all are important parts of the Thai heritage. But much more is going on.

This is an ancient culture, but it is also an emerging twentieth-century nation that is rapidly becoming modern, industrial, and international.

Both parents in a young family in Bangkok are just as likely to be working as are their counterparts in New York City or Paris. They find that the cost of living in the big city makes two incomes necessary. Like young parents in the West, they try to find a good day nursery or reliable baby-sitter to look after the children. They spend their evenings watching Thai and Western videotapes. On their vacations they travel through their country taking in the sights at national parks, famous beaches, and religious shrines.

The typical Thai university student is more interested in establishing a career and shaping a good future for his or her family than in studying the nation's exotic past. Many modern Thai families make great personal sacrifices in order to send the brightest of their sons and daughters to Europe, the United States, or Japan for further education. Ideally, they find management jobs with one of Bangkok's international corporations.

The government has made great strides in promoting education in the past few decades. Between 1960 and 1985 the number of children enrolled in government schools doubled. The adult literacy rate has climbed to more than 85 percent. The government is working toward a goal of 100 percent.

Special programs encourage modern scientific methods of farming, mining, forestry, livestock raising, and fishing. At the same time, new and diversified industries are growing in number. Incentives are offered to foreign investors to bring new industries to Thailand.

Health care is getting increased attention, too. New hospitals are being built in rural areas, where newly graduated doctors are required to serve for three years. Health education programs are taught in schools. Mobile clinics bring medical, dental, and optical services to villages.

Thailand's geographic neighbors have had a variety of unsettling political problems. This has made Thai leaders very interested in international peace and cooperation.

Their Majesties King Bhumibol and Queen Sirikit follow the example of many earlier Thai monarchs in working to raise the standard of living for all citizens. They travel a great deal throughout the nation, visiting rural areas and keeping informed by firsthand contact with the people. Education, occupational

training, public health, soil improvement, and reforestation are given high priority. The king and queen have also made trips to foreign countries to spread goodwill and interest in Thailand.

Thailand is anticipating the next century with optimism. It is taking steps to make life a little less difficult for its citizens at the bottom of the economic ladder. Also, it is encouraging tourism, the country's most lucrative industry. At the same time, it is struggling to preserve the natural resources and traditional culture that make Thailand a place of beauty.

One can only hope that, fifty years from now, visitors will still be able to enjoy the sight of friendly faces, talented dancers presenting classical drama, thousands of orchids hanging from porches, waterways crowded with picturesque craft, trained elephants performing tasks no other creature is able to do, multicolored temples glistening in the tropical sun, and people enjoying festivals in their own, uniquely Thai fashion.

MAP KEY

MINI-FACTS AT A GLANCE

GENERAL INFORMATION

Official Name: Muang Thai (Land of the Free)

Capital: Bangkok

Official Language: Thai

Other Languages: Malay and various Chinese dialects are spoken by a small number of Thai. English is widely spoken in business and government contexts.

Government: Thailand has been a constitutional monarchy since the revolution of 1932. The government is divided into executive, legislative, and judicial branches. The king, though the head of state, has little actual power. Nevertheless, he is a powerful symbol of national unity. A fourteen-member Privy Council advises him on various state matters.

The constitution of 1978 declared the king head of state and the prime minister head of the government. The National Assembly, or congress, nominates the prime minister and the king formally appoints him. The Council of Ministers, or cabinet, may have up to forty-four ministers and deputy ministers, who are selected by the prime minister.

The legislative branch of government consists of a bicameral National Assembly. The 225 members of the Senate are appointed by the prime minister with the consent of the king. The 301 members of the House of Representatives are elected by the people.

The judicial branch of government consists of three levels of courts. The *Sarn Dika*, or Supreme Court, has a chief justice and twenty-one associate justices. The king appoints these and the lower-level judges with the advice of the prime minister.

Thailand is divided into seventy-three provinces, which are further subdivided into around six hundred districts. A governor rules each province and a district officer is in charge of each district. Groups of villages are also organized into *tambols*, or communes. Leaders of each village elect one person among themselves to be the *kamnan*, or commune chief.

All Thais twenty years of age and older may vote. Several political parties are in operation in Thailand, but the Communist party is outlawed.

Flag: Thailand's flag, adopted in 1917, consists of five horizontal stripes. The two red outer stripes represent the nation, the two white inner stripes represent Buddhism, and the blue stripe in the center represents the monarchy.

Coat of Arms: Thailand's coat of arms is a representation of the Garuda, a mythical Hindu creature that is half man and half eagle.

National Anthem: *"Pleng Chart"* ("National Anthem of Thailand")

Religion: More than 95 percent of Thais are Buddhists who belong to the Hinayana, or Theravada, sect. More than 40 percent of Thai Buddhist men over the age of twenty serve in the Buddhist monkhood for at least a few months. Animism, or spirit worship, and Hindu beliefs are liberally intertwined with Buddhism in Thailand, as are the use of astrology and fortune-telling. Chinese people in Thailand practice Mahayana Buddhism, Confucianism, and Taoism. The Malays are Muslims; the Vietnamese, Mahayana Buddhists; and the Indians, Hindus. Most people of European origin are Christians.

Money: The basic monetary unit is the baht. In the summer of 1986, 26 baht were equal to one U.S. dollar.

Weights and Measures: Thailand uses the metric system.

Population: The 1986 estimated population of Thailand was 56,000,000.

Cities:

Bangkok	5,500,000
Chiang Mai	200,000
Hat Yai	125,000
Khon Kaen	125,000

(Population figures according to 1985 estimate)

GEOGRAPHY

Highest Point: Inthanon Mountain, 8,514 ft. (2,595 m)

Lowest Point: Sea level

Coastline: 1,635 mi. (2,631 km)

Mountains: In northwest Thailand are the Northern Mountains, where Doi Inthanon, the highest peak, stands. This range extends toward the south all along the western border of the country and into the Malay peninsula.

Rivers: The largest river is the Mekong, which forms the northeastern border along the Khorat Plateau. The Mekong, Chi, and Mun rivers are irrigation sources for rice farming on the plateau. The four rivers that irrigate the Central Plain—the Ping, Wang, Nan, and Yom—flow into the Chao Phraya River. The Chao Phraya runs through Bangkok and empties into the Gulf of Siam. It is Thailand's principal transportation route.

Climate: Thailand has a hot and humid climate. There are three seasons. Spring (March through May) is hot and dry. Summer (June through October) is hot and wet. Winter (November through March) is mild. The average temperature in Bangkok is 62° F. (17° C) in January and 98° F. (37° C) in May. Temperatures in the Northern Mountains are cooler, with an average January temperature of 32° F. (0° C) and an average May temperature of 90° F. (32° C).

The summer monsoons bring heavy rains from June through October. The southern peninsula receives an average of 100 in. (254 cm) of rainfall a year, compared to 55 in. (140 cm) in Bangkok.

Greatest Distances: North to south—1,100 mi. (1,770 km)
East to west—480 mi. (772 km)

Area: 198,457 sq. mi. (514,000 km²)

NATURE

Vegetation: Teak is plentiful in the Northern Mountains. There is an abundance of tropical fruit trees, such as mangoes, bananas, pineapples, and durians. Many varieties of orchids are both cultivated and found in the wild. In the rain forests of the south, about a hundred different kinds of trees can exist on a single acre, including rubber trees, bamboo, and screw pines.

Fish: Anchovies, mackerel, and shellfish are caught in the rivers and coastal waters. Many Thai farmers raise fish and shellfish in ponds on their property. Shrimp is the major fishery export.

Animals: In the forests and jungles are boars, crocodiles, deer, tigers, and poisonous snakes such as banded kraits and cobras. Tropical birds, leopards, Himalayan bears, monkeys, flying squirrels, and flying lizards are also plentiful. Domesticated water buffalo are used in agriculture. Elephants are invaluable in the logging industry, but the wild elephant population is declining seriously.

EVERYDAY LIFE

Food: Rice is eaten with almost every meal. Curries and salads made of meat, fish, and vegetables are an important part of the Thai diet. Hot peppers, garlic, and coriander are the most popular seasonings. Typical desserts are sticky rice baked with coconut sauce or fruit, banana fritters, and custards. *Kanom krok* is made of a mixture of shredded coconut, coconut milk, and other ingredients cooked over an open fire. *Look-chob* are confections shaped and decorated to look like miniature fruits and vegetables.

Housing: People in the villages live in wood or thatch houses. Houses along rivers and canals are built on stilts to be safe from flooding during the rainy season. Farm animals often sleep beneath the houses. Many people in the cities live in small wooden or stucco houses. Some live in shop houses, which are dwellings above ground-floor business establishments. Large apartment buildings are also found in cities such as Bangkok and Chiang Mai.

Holidays:

January 1, New Year's Day
Mid-February, Chinese New Year's
Early April, Songkran Day (rice festival)
April 6, Chakri Day
May 2, National Labor Day
May 5, Coronation Day
Late May/early June, Visakha Puja (Buddha's birthday)
Late July/early August, Beginning of Buddhist Lent
August 12, Queen's birthday
October 23, Chulalongkorn Day
Early November, Loi Krathong (candle ceremony on the waterways)
December 5, King's birthday
December 10, Constitution Day
December 31, New Year's Eve

Culture: Thai culture is rooted in a strong sense of family. Religion is also a major influence in Thai culture, as well as in the arts. Thai paintings and sculptures depict predominantly religious subjects, such as the Buddha and events in his life. The traditional Thai architectural style, exemplified in its ornate temples, is used in many modern non-religious buildings as well.

Sports and Recreation: A popular spectator sport is Thai-style boxing, in which opponents fight with both hands and feet. The Thai also enjoy soccer and *takraw*, a game in which players use their heads, legs, and feet to keep a wicker ball in the air. *Mak ruk*, a board game similar to chess, is also popular. Cock fights and fish fights are other favorite pastimes.

Schools: Education is valued highly in Thailand. The country boasts an 85 percent literacy rate for those over ten years old. Up until the late nineteenth century, temple monks provided children's education. Now most children attend public schools. Parents who can afford tuition send their children to private schools. Seven years of school attendance is required by law. Only about 43 percent of Thai children receive a high-school education. About 10 percent of the population has graduated from high school. Thailand has 14 universities, 43 teachers' colleges, and 179 vocational schools.

Health: Attempts are being made to raise health-care standards. Hospitals are being built, mobile clinics are being established, and young doctors are required to serve in rural areas for three years after training. Although mosquitoes abound, there are few instances of malaria. Hepatitis is fairly common, however.

ECONOMY AND INDUSTRY

Principal Products:
Agriculture: Rice, sugarcane, corn, rubber, manioc, cassava, tobacco, mushrooms, orchids
Manufacturing: Textiles, clothing, integrated circuits, processed foods, wood products, cement
Forestry: Teak, bamboo, rattan
Fishing: Shrimp and other shellfish, anchovies, mackerel
Mining: Tin, tungsten, bauxite, iron ore, lead, manganese, natural gas, precious stones, lignite

Communication: About fifty daily newspapers are published in Thailand, twenty of which are published in Bangkok. Most newspapers are in the Thai language; others are in Chinese or English. Major cities are linked by telephone and telegraph lines. There are four major television networks and over two hundred radio stations, all of which are owned and operated by the government.

Transportation: There are over 13,000 mi. (21,000 km) of paved roads in Thailand and over 2,400 mi. (3,800 km) of railroad track. A network of rivers and canals carries local passenger and cargo vessels. The largest port is Bangkok's harbor. Don Muang International Airport near Bangkok is an important port of call for flights between Thailand and cities in Asia, Australia, and Europe. The airports at Phuket and Surat Thanai are being expanded. Local airlines link Thailand's major cities.

IMPORTANT DATES

1238 — Thai kingdom is established when Thai chiefs defeat the Khmer at Sukhothai

1275-1317 — Reign of King Ramkhamhaeng

1296 — Chiang Mai is founded

1350 — King Ramathibodi establishes the kingdom of Ayutthaya, centered in the city of Ayutthaya on the Chao Phraya River

1454 — King Trailok introduces many reforms in Ayutthaya's government

1512 — The Portuguese first arrive in Ayutthaya

1569 — Burmese forces take over Ayutthaya kingdom

1584 — Naresuen challenges Burma's power in Ayutthaya

1590—Naresuen takes over Ayutthaya as king

1608—Ayutthaya sends its first ambassador to The Netherlands; Dutch traders visit Ayutthaya

1612—British traders first enter Ayutthaya

1664—King Narai allows French missionaries to establish a church in Ayutthaya

1684—Louis XIV of France sends ambassadors to Ayutthaya

1688—After attempted coup by European factions, the country is closed to foreigners for over 150 years

1767—Burmese again invade Ayutthaya and destroy the capital

1782—Rama I (Chao Phraya Chakri) establishes the Chakri dynasty, with the new capital at Bangkok; the nation takes the name of Siam

1785—Burmese invade Siam but are defeated

1809—Rama II begins a reign of peace and prosperity

1824—Rama III becomes king

1826—The British take over Burma; Rama III negotiates a Treaty of Amity and Commerce with Britain

1833—Siam and the United States form diplomatic ties

1851—Mongkut (Rama IV) comes to the throne and encourages relations with the West.

1868—Chulalongkorn (Rama V) becomes king; he abolishes slavery and establishes a system of public education

1910—Vajiravudh (Rama VI) becomes king

1917—Siam enters World War I on the side of the Allies

1925—Prajadhipok (Rama VII) ascends to the throne

1932—A coup d'état ends seven hundred years of absolute monarchy; a constitutional monarchy is established

1935—Rama VII abdicates; his ten-year-old nephew Ananda Mahidol becomes Rama VIII, but regents rule in his place

1937—Colonel Pibul Songgram assumes power

1939—Official name of the country is changed to Thailand

1941—Japan invades Thailand

1942—Thailand declares war on the U.S. and Great Britain, though it does not act on the declaration

1946—Ananda (Rama VIII) is assassinated; his brother Bhumibol Adulyadej becomes Rama IX

1950—Thailand signs a technical aid agreement with the U.S.

1954—Thailand joins the Southeast Asia Treaty Organization (SEATO)

1964—Communist terrorists begin to be active in southern Thailand

1965—U.S. uses air bases in Thailand to attack Communist forces in Southeast Asia

1967—Thailand becomes a founding member of the Association of Southeast Asian Nations (ASEAN)

1968—A new constitution provides for a bicameral legislature

1969—Martial law ends; first general elections in eleven years are held

1973—University students lead civilian revolt against the government; a series of democratically elected governments follows

1975—Thailand establishes diplomatic relations with China

1976—Conservative groups attack and subdue radical student groups; military groups again take over the government

1978—A new constitution is instituted

1980—Retired General Prem Tinsulanonda becomes prime minister

1981—Prime Minister Prem Tinsulanonda supresses an attempted military coup

1983—National elections are held

1986—King Bhumibol becomes longest reigning king of the Chakri dynasty

IMPORTANT PEOPLE

King Bhumibol Adulyadej (b. 1927), Rama IX; king of Thailand since 1946

Chao Phraya Chakri, founder of the Chakri dynasty in 1782; took the title Rama I

Chulalongkorn (r. 1868-1910), Rama V; Thai monarch who modernized the government and established many social reforms

Mongkut (r. 1851-1868), Rama IV; one of Siam's most influential monarchs; nurtured Siam's relations with foreign powers

Narai (r. 1657-1688), king of Ayutthaya; under his reign the French attempted to subvert the royal power; over a century and a half of anti-foreign sentiment followed

Naresuen, Thai king who recaptured Ayutthaya from the Burmese in 1590

Pibul Songgram, military officer who ruled Thailand from 1937 to 1944 and served as prime minister until 1957; sided with Japan during World War II

Prajadhipok (r. 1925-1935), Rama VII; Thai king during the Great Depression; abdicated when a coup d'état changed the government to a constitutional monarchy

Prem Tinsulanonda, prime minister of Thailand since 1980

Ramathibodi, prince who became king and founded the kingdom of Ayutthaya in 1350

Ramkhamhaeng (r. 1275-1317), powerful Sukhothai ruler; invented the Thai alphabet; enlarged and consolidated the Siamese kingdom and introduced many social reforms

Sarit Thanarat, military officer who ruled Thailand from 1957 to 1963; brought extensive economic development to Thailand and strengthened ties with the United States

Queen Sirikit, present queen of Thailand

Boromo Trailok (r. 1448-1488), Thai king who introduced many government reforms

Thanom Kittikachorn, Thai prime minister from 1963 to 1973, a time marked by demonstrations, coups, and other political unrest

Prince Wachiralongkon, son of King Bhumibol and Queen Sirikit; invested as crown prince of Thailand in 1972

INDEX

Page numbers that appear in boldface type indicate illustrations.

125

About the Author

Sylvia McNair was born in Korea, daughter of Methodist missionaries. A graduate of Oberlin College, she is the author of several travel books published by Rand McNally and Company and Fisher Travel Guides. Her articles on travel, education, and other subjects have appeared in numerous magazines. In addition to her free-lance work, she is a partner in an Evanston, Illinois, firm called Editorial/Research Service.

Ms. McNair has been active in various professional and community organizations. She was a founding member of Chicago Women in Publishing, has served on the national board of the Society of American Travel Writers, and was elected to two terms on a district school board. She has three sons, one daughter, and two grandsons.

Ms. McNair would like to acknowledge the assistance and consultation of several Thai students attending Roosevelt University in Chicago, especially Varakorn Mangclasiri.